WHOLEHEARTED LEADERSHIP REVOLUTION

LEARN HOW 10 IMPACTFUL MEN AND WOMEN HAVE DISRUPTED WORN OUT METHODS TO LEAD THROUGH CRISIS AND BUILD MOMENTUM

Wholehearted Leadership Revolution

Published by Wholehearted Publications
in association with Four Eagles Publishing

First published in Australia in 2023
Copyright © 2023 Wholehearted Publications
All rights reserved.

No part of this book may be reproduced in
any form or by any electronic or mechanical
means, including information storage and
retrieval systems without written permission
from the author, except for the use of brief
quotations in a book review. Requests
to the publisher should be directed to
support@foureaglespublishing.com

The information in this book is the author's
opinion only. Readers should not rely on
the general information given in this book
as a substitute for professional advice.
The author and publisher cannot accept
responsibility for any losses, damages or
adverse effects that may result from the
use of information contained in this book.

A catalogue record for this book is available
from the National Library of Australia

ISBN 978-0-6458469-6-6

Wholehearted Leadership Revolution

CONTENTS

INTRODUCTION 1

ANDREW RAMSDEN 11
    Logic is the Beginning of Wisdom, Not the End
    About the Author 25

ROB KIRBY 27
    The Power of Paradox in Performance
    About the Author 39

FEDA ADRA 41
    The Why Behind Meaningful Connections
    About the Author 51

DAVID BEAL 53
    The Art of Doing Nothing
    About the Author 65

CHERYL CRUTTENDEN 67
    BE Out Standing in Your Field
    About the Author 83

MARTIN KRIPPNER 85
    The Case for Volunteer Leadership: Getting the Best from Others When They're Not Obliged to Try
    About the Author 99

Wholehearted Leadership Revolution

ANDREW LIZZIO 101
> *Shining Brightly*
>
> About the Author 119

NICKY MIH 121
> *A Book, a Promise and a Mission of Epic Proportions*
>
> About the Author 133

SARAH-JANE PERSCHLINGMANN 135
> *Stepping into My Power; Leading with Heart*
>
> About the Author 147

JOHN SMILEK 149
> *Values in Leadership and Life*
>
> About the Author 159

Wholehearted Leadership Revolution

INTRODUCTION

The world is evolving. And right now, as you read this, its evolution is accelerating. Can you feel it? This tectonic shift in the pace of our change started with the introduction of the Digital Age and it is getting faster every day, as we enter the Age of Artificial Intelligence (AI).

But even though the speed of change is at an all-time high, it's currently the slowest it will ever be again. Technology has made each of our individual worlds bigger while, at the same time, making the globe feel smaller. It has provided many new ways to stay connected, and yet so many feel more isolated and lonelier than before. It has made many aspects of our lives easier while adding incredible complexity that makes large-scale change more difficult. How can the world be at once bigger and smaller? More connected and yet more isolating? Easier and yet more difficult?

Confusing, isn't it?

As the world has become more connected, the various people, cultures and subcultures of the world have mingled, exposing us to very different sets of perspectives and values. In the past, we would have just 'gone along with our tribe,' but now that we have so many tribes in the mix, we have to consider that these tensions and paradoxes will no longer just go away. This has led to growing polarisation and conflict in our modern world.

Paradox, complexity and accelerating change are at the heart of our personal and global pain. In the modern world, we are expected to make sense of these perplexing tensions that pervade every aspect of our lives. Consider the following common examples.

- We can lose weight on a no-carb diet or an all-carb diet. So are carbohydrates good or bad?

- We want to be loved passionately and unconditionally, but if we dote too much on our partner we are considered 'clingy' or 'needy' and may be pushed away. So is loving others right or wrong? And is there such a thing as too much love?
- Too much screen time for children means they may end up with a short attention span; not enough and they won't build important skills or be able to relate to their social peers. So should we let them spend time on screens or not?
- We know we need to give critical feedback and have courageous conversations, but at the same time we're expected to be compassionate and hold space for others. So do we listen, speak our truth or sugar-coat it?
- We know we need to celebrate the small wins and that being relaxed leads to greater innovation, but we're expected to always be striving, delivering and improving. So is it really okay to ever give ourselves a little space and enjoy our work?
- You can be passionate and committed but risk becoming frustrated and burn out. So is being Wholehearted really a great strategy?

This list could go on and on.

We are tempted to label the opposing sides of these dilemmas as 'right' or 'wrong', and situations, people and things as 'good' or 'bad', yet the truth is *never* that black and white. Paradoxically, the only absolute position I can defend is that all absolute positions are fundamentally flawed.

Have you ever thought *It's all insert-politician-here's fault!* Or maybe you've thought something like *Big corporations are to blame. Many are suffering while they become ridiculously wealthy*-or some other variation of 'insert big bad politician, government, corporation, industry, elite-cabal here'? Yes, people make poor decisions, some more than others, and yet to focus blame on a single person, company or thing is an over-simplification that misses the larger truth: The wicked problems we face as a society are systemic and require a more nuanced understanding.

So why then do we tend to simplify and point the finger of blame so readily? Because it helps us resolve *uncertainty*.

The only thing worse than feeling like there's some great evil out there trying to ruin things for us everyday people is uncertainty. It is as though we are allergic to it! We avoid and limit uncertainty at all costs, even if we must suffer through sadness, frustration or rage towards whoever or whatever we've identified as the source of the problem. It feels better to blame with confidence than to admit we don't know who to blame. Or worse, to acknowledge that, at some level, we might all be to blame.

This aversion to uncertainty leads us to make quick judgements about what's right and wrong. We may be tempted to back the underdog instead of the people in power, the long-term thinker in preference to the short-term thinker, or the altruist who is trying to do the right thing for all. However, it turns out that the truth is much harder to live with: the world is an incredibly complex system of systems, built on hierarchies and incentives, which have driven our evolution over time. In fact, the underdog may be no better than the incumbent, the long-term thinker may struggle to understand what's important about living here and now, and the one who looks out for others may self-sacrifice to the point of frustration, resentment, passive-aggressive attacks and even rage.

It's also tempting to believe that we always make the 'right choices' and yet history suggests that, given the wrong circumstances, we are all capable of making less-than-stellar choices, choices that hurt others, or even ourselves. Heavy, isn't it? It takes great personal courage to face this not-so-pleasant truth.

I encourage you to take a deep breath and stick with me for one more paragraph of hard truth, for even heavy feelings have great power.

Finally, it's tempting to believe that we're making the 'right choices' *right now*. But is that the reality of things? Could there be great injustices in the world that we all tolerate, ignore and even benefit from? Sadly, the answer is 'yes.' You need only search online for 'cobalt mining in the Congo' to discover how human rights abuses keep us supplied with batteries for our electric cars, our trillions of mobile devices, and even the laptop I'm using to type this very sentence.

I don't mention all of this to make anyone feel bad. And if you do, take another deep breath and as you let it go, forgive yourself, *right now*. Guilt and shame will not help us make progress. I mention all of this only to illustrate how complex we are, and therefore how complex the challenges are that we face as a global society. We built the systems around us, we're part of them and we benefit greatly from them. This means we all contribute to the problems in our lives and in the world, either actively or by turning a blind eye. *Not easy to own!* The good news is that by owning our part in the problems, we can now also be part of the solutions. This is key to Wholeheartedness. This is how we take our power back.

We can turn injustice and suffering around. Every one of us can contribute towards a brighter future for ourselves, for those around us, our children and the world. None of this is insurmountable or overwhelming. It just requires as many of us as possible to step up and be Wholehearted in our own lives, in our careers or businesses, and in society more broadly. How many? Research shows as little as ten per cent of the population (if they remain committed) need to adopt new ideas and principles in order to influence all the rest.

Here's where it gets really exciting. The solution doesn't have to be through grand interventions or major achievements. As you'll read in this book, even small gestures add up and collect scale and momentum, like a snowball rolling downhill. A small change in the right place is all that's needed to trigger a positive systemic shift. Because you're reading this, I believe that you have what it takes to start that snowball rolling.

Have you ever felt the following:

- jaded, over it, disheartened or defeated;
- exhausted, or as though you only live for the weekends;
- the need to play politics or just keep your head down;
- that there are 'painful people', or situations better avoided if possible;

- as though you're just doing what you're doing for a payday, or for the perks;
- that you have to force your purpose to align with your organisation's vision;
- or that it's not worth even allowing yourself to have a big vision for your life or your impact on the world because it's just too hard?

I suspect we have all experienced these feelings at some point in our careers and lives. I've certainly felt all of them. These are clues that we're either not listening to our hearts, or we're finding reasons not to follow the heart's guidance. It ultimately means we're living our lives half-heartedly, or sometimes even with a closed heart. This ultimately prevents us from getting the best from ourselves and those around us.

Not only is this extremely common, but there are many good reasons we can fall into these patterns and start to close our hearts. For example, following our hearts can get us into trouble because this requires us to put our true selves out there, for which we may come under fire. It also requires us to question and even challenge the systems around us and can therefore put our income and stability at risk.

But ultimately, more and more Wholehearted Leaders are realising that it's worth it. It's better than living a life of quiet regret. It's the best way to expand ourselves and our influence and to live a life of which we are proud, to make a bigger positive impact and to leave the world a better place than we found it.

If you're reading this book, I'm sure you can relate to the above paradoxes and frustrations. You're the type of person who likes to excel in your work or business and feel good doing it. You're well placed to lead others, and you're likely already doing that on a small or large scale. Most of all, there's an inner voice or feeling that speaks to you softly (or perhaps loudly) that is ill-at-ease with different aspects of what's happening in the world. You already take action to make it a better place and yet you still want to be able to make an even bigger positive impact. Does this sound like you? Good, you're in the right place.

Imagine a world where, no matter the scale of the challenges in front of you, you never have to feel uncertain. In this world, you don't have to worry about office politics, hidden agendas, setbacks, or failure. Indeed, the waves of change and depths of complexity aren't overwhelming anymore but, instead, become just the ocean upon which you set sail, and can be broken down and tackled one fathom at a time.

Imagine if you felt like this.

Wholehearted Leaders feel a sense of purpose and focus that lights their way. They don't sweat the petty games that others play. They back themselves to be able to handle whatever comes their way and move forwards with confidence. Where others would catastrophise, Wholehearted Leaders know that even failure and defeat are temporary if you have grit and persistence.

If you asked the authors in this book, "Do you feel like this all the time?", or "Do you get it right every time?", I'm sure they'd answer, "We do not." And yet Wholehearted Leaders face everything as it comes, with compassion for themselves and others, and courage and faith that they will find a way through.

If you felt like this *most* days, wouldn't your life be forever changed?

It's said we tend to overestimate what we can achieve in a year and underestimate what we can achieve in three or more years. What challenges could you tackle over time if you felt this way? To get the most out of life, our careers and businesses, we must feel this way! Being Wholehearted is the key to maximising the positive outcomes for ourselves and for others around us as well.

This is the difference that Wholehearted Leaders make in our world. They hold the complexity, uncertainty and chaos inherent in our modern life and make a positive difference that not only benefits themselves and those like them, but also takes the best from all perspectives and finds the most beneficial way forward for humanity as a whole.

So what does it mean to be Wholehearted anyway?

It's a many-faceted concept. In this book, each author contributes his or her unique perspective and experience and yet there will be themes that will start to emerge. Some of these themes include key superpowers that Wholehearted Leaders develop, for example:

- an ability to focus and follow through with commitment and courage even in the face of paradox and complexity;
- an ability to face all of humanity-the good, the bad and the ugly with compassion for all; and
- the ability to lead with not only the head but the heart as well.

As a result, Wholehearted Leaders are able to hold all perspectives, hear all truths, embrace both sides of every polarity, *take the best* from each and leave the rest, all while honouring the core values upon which their lives are built. This is how we will address the challenges we face in the modern world personally, locally, nationally and globally.

Wholehearted Leaders allow themselves to dream big about the kind of impact they want to have in the world. They make sure the vision of the organisation for which they work aligns with their personal purpose (not the other way around). And they are *all in,* 100 per cent, both feet and everything else. This commitment to their purpose, above anything else, frees them up to follow their hearts and do what needs to be done, including questioning those systems around them that need to be questioned.

As a result, Wholehearted Leaders attract and inspire followers at a rate that is the envy of other leaders. Their passion and commitment motivate others to find their own passion and contribute discretionary effort to the shared cause. Wholehearted Leaders are out there challenging the unchecked growth of systems, organisations and even our consumption, where it will put our societies at risk. In this way, they are courageous, persistent and resilient, and inspire those same qualities in others.

In this Wholehearted philosophy, you'll hear echoes of Integral Theory, Teal Organisations and Metamodernism. These are all incredibly useful frameworks, and yet they need further support, examples and practical tools to help understand and embody the Wholehearted Leadership approach. We aim to deliver some of these through this very book. After all, being Wholehearted is ultimately a *feeling*. It's this feeling that provides us with the foundation to achieve everything we desire and overcome the challenges that crop up along the way.

Did you know feelings had this kind of power?

Ever 'get up on the wrong side of the bed'? This well-known saying makes it clear. When we are in a bad mood everything seems harder; we rub others the wrong way, trigger conflicts, and find it much easier to be frustrated by the world. We feel overwhelmed and may even catastrophise and give up. *Into the too-hard basket!*

This is the *power of feeling*. When you can embody the unique emotional cocktail of your own Wholehearted feeling, have a strong inner container to retain that feeling most days and the ability to restore it when you face obstacles and setbacks, then you'll unlock your own Wholehearted superpowers.

Feelings are notoriously difficult to describe because they are subjective, the domain of our emotional subconscious mind. The best way to communicate with these parts of ourselves is through symbols, metaphors and stories. Our hope is that you'll read the journeys, struggles and emotions of each author in this book and perhaps you'll identify with the challenges they've overcome. A particular story, message, or insight may resonate with you, and you will be able to take away what is most powerful for you and your next steps. In other words, you'll *take the best and leave the rest*. In doing so you will start to define what being Wholehearted feels like to you. Hold onto that feeling and it will serve you incredibly well, as it has served the authors of this book.

In other words, the Revolution starts *within*.

The Wholehearted journey is one I've been on, in one way or another, most of my life. Whether I knew it at the time or not, there was something inside me searching for a better way to lead my life, career and business. Maybe you can relate? This journey was greatly accelerated for me over the past decade by the events you'll read about in my chapter, and from the teachings of my mentor, Rob Kirby, who has been on this journey much longer than I have. It's fair to say that for both of us the journey isn't over, and yet it has already made such a significant impact on the quality of our lives, for those we lead and for our clients—over 40,000 so far between us. So we knew it was time to share this message with the world in the form of a book.

However, such a complex concept that requires the integration of many perspectives would not make sense if written by only two people. No, for this book to work we agreed it would require the voices of others on the Wholehearted Leadership path.

I met each of the authors in this book in different contexts and parts of the world over the past 15 years or so. They have been very special colleagues, mentors, business partners, podcast guests, conference speakers or serendipitous introductions. What draws them together for me is the impact their presence and their journeys have had on me and many others. I feel incredibly blessed to have all of them come together and share their stories and insights in this book. We don't have all the answers- for that we would all have to work together. What we do offer are pieces of the overarching framework and pathway forwards.

The authors in this book have all achieved incredible things in their industries and careers and are making a real difference for those around them. Most importantly, they follow their hearts and go *all in* to realise their vision for the world. They have each questioned basic assumptions inherent in the systems around us and, in doing so, have found new ways to deal with challenges and paradoxes that others have struggled to overcome. I personally found all of the stories in this book powerful, moving, insightful and inspirational.

These authors are in the vanguard of this modern approach known as Wholehearted Leadership, but they aren't alone. And this is key- the more of us there are working together, the easier it all gets. It's an exciting time in history as many more are becoming curious about being heart-centred, heart-led and heartfelt in their leadership. If that's you then I know you'll get a lot from this book, so please enjoy, and ...

Welcome to the **Wholehearted Leadership Revolution!**

Andrew Ramsden

ANDREW RAMSDEN

Logic is the Beginning of Wisdom, Not the End

Why don't I feel anything? I wondered to myself, confused. *No time for naval gazing now.* I snapped myself back to the present and looked down at my daughter, still damp, and inordinately red, nestled in my arms with a blanket draped around us. Under the blanket she was resting on my bare chest so she felt skin-to-skin contact during her first minutes on earth. "Hey, Mira. Welcome to the world." I have tears welling up in my eyes as I write this, and yet at the time, I felt nothing.

I should be feeling something, my mind raced, self-judgement kicking in. A nurse appeared in my peripheral vision. "Are you okay, Dad?" "Yes, all good," I responded in a flat monotone. It was a lie, even if I felt nothing I knew logically I wasn't 'all good'. But I was good enough for the job at hand, and she couldn't help me anyway. I looked up as she turned quickly away onto the next task. There were at least ten medical personnel buzzing around the room, maybe 15. I didn't have the mental bandwidth to count, all I knew was it seemed like an alarming number, or at least it should have felt that way. *Where did they all come from so quickly?*

As I scanned the room, I could see my wife sprawled naked on a hospital bed bleeding, with doctors and nurses moving around her like an F1 pit crew. Nothing. Beside the bed I see the water-birthing tub, only minutes earlier a beautiful shrine to the miracle of birth, surrounded with LED candles and our vision board, gentle music playing to welcome our daughter into the world. Now a sea the colour of claret, it turns my stomach to think about it as I write, but in that moment, nada.

Why am I numb? I thought I was past this! Self-judgement turned to a sense of frustration. At this point I felt inhuman. And yet I knew if Mira didn't feel welcomed and safe right now, she would spend her life feeling disconnected from the world as well. *It's now or never, Dad.* I gave myself an ultimatum, I knew what I had to do.

I took a moment to focus back in on me and my body first, my breathing, the feeling of my feet on the floor. I scrunched my toes around in my shoes, picked up my knees one at a time and thumped my heels down into the floor. Finally, I forgave myself for being numb and for buying into the misunderstanding that this experience should be felt a certain way. As grounding routines go it wouldn't win any awards, but it would have to be enough. *I am here.*

I looked down at the tiny child curled up in my arms, and at that moment she opened her eyes and calmly looked back up at me. And I felt it. A deep sense of connection like somehow I'd known her my whole life. "Hello, darling. Daddy's here and I'm not going anywhere. I love you with all my heart, and I always will. I've got you."

That was four months ago. I'm sure you'll be pleased to hear Baby Bear and Mama Bear are doing really well, thanks to the amazing medical professionals and our doula, Jacki. I've heard a number of people say, "Having children was the best thing I ever did." I used to think this sentiment was a bit overblown, because I've had some pretty amazing experiences in life and I'm sure they have too. But now I get it. And I agree, which would be rather surprising for someone who knew me five years ago. For most of my life, I was dead against having children. So much so that I chose to have a vasectomy in my early thirties (I'm 41 now). It's not that I didn't like children, I just didn't trust the world I would be bringing them into. To be more specific, I didn't trust the *people* in that world.

You see, to be brutally honest with you and with myself... there's a part of me that hates everyone.

Other parts of me disagree, so, while I would find it very hard to 'push the button', if the world did come to a cataclysmic conclusion at the expense of all humanity, that part of me suspects we would probably deserve it.

For ease of reference, let's call that part of me 'Scott'. No, I don't have multiple personalities but, like all of us, I have a range of sub-personalities. Have you ever felt conflicted, as if there are different internal voices or feelings when faced with an important decision? For most of my life I wasn't aware of these different influences within me but, sure enough, once you notice them, there they are. For example, there's the part that feels small sometimes, like a child, it frightens easily and loves to play. There's also a part of me that holds myself to a very high standard and can sometimes be quite harsh and critical. And yet another that desperately wants it all to mean something, and to make a positive difference in the world. I'm sure you can relate to one or more of these-we're complicated, aren't we?

Scott was repeatedly drawn to zombie films and other post-apocalyptic fantasies. There's a simplicity to that life: no more office politics, no more keeping up with the Joneses or trying to impress others. No more asking the question *How can I do better next time?* And no more suspense waiting to see if we can avoid a collision of modern crises. In that world, the catastrophe has already happened.

I figured that after the apocalypse we need only focus on the base levels of Maslow's Hierarchy of Needs: air, water, food, shelter, and to protect and provide for family. Simple. But if you've ever watched any zombie series such as *The Walking Dead* or *The Last of Us,* you'll notice a common thread: the zombies are a nuisance, but the real threat quickly becomes-that's right-other humans. And we're back. Even in a post-apocalyptic world there's no escaping the truth: humans are a problem.

Scott would say, "Humans are *the* problem." He believed this from the start and was always on the lookout for examples to justify his belief. But he didn't have to rely on fictional universes to justify that position, as I grew up it was all around.

I found school anxiety-provoking, literally. So much so, in first grade, I would blink uncontrollably, like a nervous tic. I hadn't even realised I was doing this until the older kids started giving me grief about it, calling me 'Blinky Bill' and pushing me around. They say the best way to deal with a bully is to not react, but I couldn't help myself. I felt a deep sadness.

I sobbed and asked them to stop, which only meant they leaned into the joke more.

It took many years to realise the blinking was caused by social anxiety. To me it was all I knew, so it just felt 'normal'. The teasing didn't feel normal. I cried every day. I just wanted to fit in, and I had the distinct feeling I did not.

I had no idea what was causing the blinking or what to do about it. My parents took me to doctors and specialists, but they didn't have a solution either. Eventually, I intuitively worked out a way to forcibly stop blinking and also dull the anxiety and sadness. I now know this was garden-variety emotional suppression, a strategy that I came to lean on so heavily over the years it would become my 'autopilot' setting, my default way of being. I had learned to numb myself.

By the time I was in high school, the bullying had escalated to forms of emotional and physical torture and general isolation. I had a small number of friends, but I also had a clear sense that, in general, I was not thought highly of. I would sometimes catch people talking about me behind my back, which was obviously not pleasant to overhear. One conversation stood out above the rest. On a school camping trip when I was 16, I heard two students talking about me with something approaching empathy. One said to the other, "I'd hate to be Andrew. It must be really tough to be him." The other agreed. Even though they had compassion for me, it was clear they weren't going to reach out and connect with me. No, that would be social suicide. For some reason to be pitied in this way hit me harder than any of the physical abuse. Something about knowing that there were people who cared, and yet even they couldn't be seen with me cut deep. So close, and yet so far.

Given this emotional legacy, it's no wonder Scott held onto his resentment and even hatred towards humanity.

I felt a great sense of injustice. I believed I was a 'nice young man'. Every movie, story and teacher I had learned from growing up stressed how important it was to be 'good' and 'nice', so, in theory, I should have been the one coming out on top. This was also how I was raised. As the oldest of five children, it was my role to set a good example for my younger siblings. So, in general, I was well-behaved, kind and generous to people. At least to their face.

Deep down I couldn't help but resent and feel jealous of others, their friendships, in-jokes and cliques. Deep down, I hated them for it and to cope with the rejection my ego had to make *them* the problem. I judged them for being too rude, too crude, too masculine, too selfish, too sexualised, whatever I could justify to myself to make myself feel better. Yes, I was judging them and even though I hid it as best I could, they could tell. Which made the problem worse. Now they resented me and pushed me further away. And even though this was a self-fulfilling prophecy, Scott was only too happy to use it as more evidence of what he already knew and he'd smugly remind me, *I told you so.*

Ironically, in my high school years I also started to find solace as a musician performing in different musical groups. It wasn't just that I was reasonably good at it, or that it was fun. There was something about playing my part in a group, and feeling my performance resonate in harmony with others that was so powerful. It felt like I fit in somewhere. In hindsight, it makes perfect sense doesn't it? Me, a chronic outcast, was yearning to be part of a team.

It was for this reason I also fell in love with *Star Trek*, which is set in a future where the world has evolved past the need for money, petty competition and even war and come together to focus on pure exploration and discovery. I watched as many episodes from different *Star Trek* series as I could borrow from my local library on VHS. I was so obsessed, I'm embarrassed to admit I spent a significant portion of my adult life with sideburns shaved to a point because *Star Trek* characters often wore them like that.

The crew of a *Star Trek* starship never fought with each other (unless possessed by aliens), and they resolved any tensions by talking to each other which strengthened their bonds. This was the world I wanted to be a part of.

In particular, I was very drawn to the 'Vulcans', a wise alien race who partnered closely with humans. The most notable Vulcan is called 'Spock', have you heard of him? The Vulcans seemed to have it all worked out-the problem was emotions and so they looked down their noses at humanity for being so emotionally driven. They believed in suppressing all emotions and instead valued only logic and rational analysis. I could relate-I'd been doing that from a young age. After all, what had emotions ever done for me but bring me pain, loneliness and sadness? This was the justification I needed to go all-in on logic and continue to push emotions down for good.

And as strategies go, it didn't *not* work. Most of the time I was able to appear unfazed by what was going on around me and appeared rational in my decisions. This served me well as I entered the workforce. As I worked my way up the corporate ladder I became known for being cool, calm and collected, even under fire or in stress-provoking situations. Combined with my conscientious 'nice guy' approach and my passion for making the world a better place, I was able to make allies, secure opportunities and kick goals.

I was also able to work my way up into executive positions, overseeing significant portfolios and large-scale digital transformation initiatives to make it easier for people to get the services they needed.

And I loved it. I felt like I fit in somewhere, and that I was making a positive difference in the world. I was also able to provide a place for others to fit in the teams under me. My aim was to nurture an environment for my teams, programs and partners like on the Starship Enterprise where trust and mutual respect were a given foundation.

But not everyone would meet me halfway. There were always some partners who took a more selfish and devious approach. These people didn't follow the unspoken rules, they didn't play nice. In my mind they played *dirty*. Their games were office politics and manipulation, which they played well. At the time I didn't have the tools to effectively manage these individuals or my own emotional response to them, so they caused me a great deal of frustration and angst, which, of course, I then suppressed.

These 'painful people' received all of Scott's attention and became the targets of his barely suppressed rage. From time to time, this pent-up emotion would slip out. Usually in small ways-some frustration here, some less-than-even tone there. People noticed. When you're known for being cool, calm and collected, any small emotional blips are quite obvious. I did my best to hide how I was really feeling, but as my career advanced, the pressure increased and my stockpile of frustration and resentment grew. There was only so much I could override.

I remember one particularly painful individual who had been causing one of my teams a great deal of unnecessary pain for months, much of which I shielded them from, but it was wearing me down. What triggered me the most was his use of dishonest logic, aka 'fallacies of argumentative reasoning'. He would twist your words around, put words in your mouth, and steamroll over anything you said in response. The problem is that it was working. People seemed to buy into his bullshit. He was a master at creating a sense of uncertainty and fear in the other executives and stakeholders and then pinning it all on us. Could no one else tell that he was making a mountain from a molehill and using flawed logic and emotional manipulation to do it? How ironic that logic was letting me down, and his fear-based emotional arguments were winning.

This all came to a head in a board meeting where his usual BS extravaganza was escalating to new heights and threatening to shut down my program completely. I felt my blood start to boil and that warmth creep up my neck and into my cheeks. "You're so dishonest, twisting my words around and blowing this completely out of proportion!" I yelled across the boardroom table in front of the other executives, including my boss's boss. I shocked myself and everyone else in the room. As a self-identified pacifist I was even more shocked to discover that if I'd let Scott off the chain in that moment I would have leapt across the table and punched this guy in the face, possibly repeatedly. Not my finest moment. But not really that surprising when you consider he was a bully- you can imagine how I felt about bullies.

Keeping a lid on Scott and my emotions, in general, was taking its toll in other ways. I was exhausted. In the evenings after work I would crash, no energy to do anything other than watch TV while comfort-eating until I passed out, usually on the couch. Then it invaded my weekends as well. I couldn't bring myself to do much at all other than work and recover.

Yes, I was working a lot, often 12 to 16 hours a day, six or seven days a week. I was passionate and loved that I was making a positive difference. I saw light at the end of the tunnel. I figured at some point it would get easier, that I wouldn't have to push myself like this forever. But I should have known the light at the end of my tunnel wasn't daylight.

Near the end of 2014 my teams had delivered a number of major projects simultaneously and I took some long overdue leave. My body had faithfully served me and now it saw its opportunity. I crashed once again but this time I didn't bounce back. For six weeks I struggled to even get out of bed.

Recovery was a long road. It took four years just to get a clear diagnosis. During those years I sought help from countless specialists, integrated and functional doctors, naturopaths and complementary medicine practitioners, coaches, therapists and healers. I changed my lifestyle, my diet, I even started exercising for the first time in my life. I tried yoga, meditation, breath work, ice baths and any number of supplements and regimes-you name it, I tried it. Much of it helped in small ways but ultimately I was still not the same. I took long service leave and used the time to start my business, which was doing really well initially. This gave me time and flexibility to focus on recovery. After four years I was lucky to be referred to an excellent doctor who specialised in thinking outside the traditional Western medical box. After running all the usual tests, he decided to test my adrenal glands. He discovered my cortisol levels were very low so he was able to give me a clear diagnosis, 'Cortisol Insufficiency' and a treatment plan of 'Hormone Replacement Therapy': take these pills four times a day, for the rest of your life. And they definitely helped. The brain fog was replaced with a sense of being wired and tired like the 'caffeine hangover' feeling you get after staying up all night and drinking two triple espressos just without the good part where you actually get to drink the coffee. This was combined with a 'fried' feeling, like there was a loose wire in between my ears that would short out painfully against my grey matter from time to time.

I tried to feel positive and grateful for this outcome, I truly did. But my energy, immune system and general state of health was still incredibly unreliable. I could only work for four hours a day without incurring a 'fatigue debt' I'd have to pay back later. And worse, I needed to take recovery days at short notice, feeling rundown and sick was common. It felt impossible to commit to action and know I could follow through. I was fundamentally a compromised version of me, I felt like I had a disability. My business needed more time and energy than I could give it so I was slipping backwards, eating my way through my savings and racking up debt. *How could I continue a career or run a business like this?!* I was distraught.

I felt like giving up. I had finally found my 'fit' and felt valued but now these were in the process of being taken from me. I was under financial pressure and didn't know how I would recover. I felt like the victim of some cruel prank from the universe and I wondered if it was my lot in life to be bullied by the universe itself. Self-pity is never a good thing, and yet when you're stuck in it, there doesn't seem to be any other way to look at the world. In a desperate attempt to understand the joke the universe clearly wasn't letting me in on, I turned to philosophy. Only Nihilism resonated with my current state of mind- the belief that nothing matters so you may as well make the most of it anyway or commit suicide, dealer's choice. I chose the former, and it helped for a while, but ultimately felt hollow. I craved meaning and yet I couldn't find it. I considered the ultimate escape. I'd been trying to escape reality in one way or another my whole life, so why not? It was a dark time for me.

It now seems so crazy that I had turned 'not being able to continue to work myself to the bone' into the end of my world. Many people live noble and courageous lives in the face of far greater challenges than mine. And yet, losing this major part of my identity meant the whole narrative and the meaning of my life felt like it had fallen away and I had no way of making sense of it. I now know how significant that is. As humans, we can endure incredible hardship and thrive if it *makes sense*. Not just at an intellectual level, it must be a *deeply felt* sense that every event, even the difficult ones, have a purpose. Senseless struggle, senseless suffering, and senseless loss are the hardest to bear. Unfortunately, no one can make sense of it for us. Ultimately, we have to *decide* it's meaningful, find the gift within the pain and have faith that it's true, then it can become deeply felt. The more significant your pain, the more difficult this is to do, however, if you are able to process it, you can emerge from any hardship stronger than before.

No one can make sense of your hardships for you, but I was lucky to discover there are some people who can help guide you through the complicated knots of stress and difficult emotions we end up in and the emotional legacy that led to them.

During the trials and tribulations of my recovery, I had the great fortune to stumble upon a number of brilliant coaches who helped me understand that my fatigue may have a physical explanation but that it was also just a symptom. The true cause was my own relationship with stress, with emotions, with others, and ultimately my relationship with myself.

And they were right. As I worked with them to process my emotional legacy—all the heavy emotions I was holding onto and suppressing—I started to feel lighter, and more of my energy returned. This time, for good.

Not only did my energy return but many of the things I had found difficult or uncomfortable got much easier. You see, I had been repeating the strategies I'd learned as a young person for dealing with pressure, emotions, and with other people. I was unconsciously recreating the same patterns over and over and bringing much of my emotional legacy into every situation, all day (for example, the bullies in the boardroom). Then when those emotions resurfaced, I'd use even more energy to suppress them again and hope that was the end of it. Exhausting!

Why was I doing this? Without realising it, we all do this in different ways and to different extents. We all have an emotional legacy. We all have a 'subconscious autopilot' programmed when we are young that heavily influences and, in many cases, outright controls our responses to everyday situations (just like you can walk or drive a car without even thinking about it). We all make situations mean more than they need to and most of us will catastrophise situations at times, feel overwhelmed or like giving up.

By doing this work I was able to wean myself off the Hormone Replacement Therapy, and my energy has returned to the levels I had in my early 20s. I now feel my emotions, but the difficult or uncomfortable emotions are far less frequent and far less intense. When they come I can process them quickly and let them go, which means I am now generally cool, calm and collected without suppression. I feel like I can face any person, situation or challenge with confidence and know I can handle pressure without turning it into stress.

I access passion and joy on a daily basis that I wouldn't have allowed myself in the past. It's transformed and supercharged not only my health and energy, but my business, my relationships, both romantic and professional, and my own personal sense of fulfilment in life.

I am now capable of holding much greater complexity, uncertainty and pressure, without turning it into stress. This is because my comfort zone has been effectively and permanently expanded by doing the inner work. I have the tools to expand it further each time I find a new area of discomfort. This means my tendency to procrastinate and avoid difficult tasks, conversations and people is vastly reduced, making me far more effective and confident as a leader, a partner and a father.

I am incredibly grateful to the coaches who helped me unlock this new chapter of my life. It had such an impact on me that I continued on to study under six of them to learn a suite of skills and modalities including Neuro-Linguistic Programming, Matrix Therapies and Body Psychotherapy, so I could help clients transform themselves as well. I now work with leaders who are facing similar challenges to those I faced to achieve their peak performance and sustainable success in business and in their lives. The breakthroughs I've facilitated are beyond what I would have logically thought possible. As I'm sure you can imagine, I take great pleasure in seeing them go on to create teams that perform like a starship crew and deliver amazing outcomes. I feel incredibly honoured to be able to pay this gift forward to others, including providing the vision and container for the leaders in this book to bring their message of Wholehearted Leadership to the world.

Most powerfully of all, doing this inner work helped me to process my relationship with humanity and let go of that bitterness, resentment and fear I had stored up. Scott is still there, but he's no longer upset. Instead, there's a whole new side to Scott I hadn't appreciated before-a truly innocent, playful and curious side that not only sees the worst in people, but sees the best in them too, and wants to work with them to build a better world, together.

The kicker is even though Scott was subconsciously shaping so much of how I felt and acted, for most of my life I wasn't even consciously aware of his existence. If you'd told me I clearly had that anger and hatred in me, I would have denied it, honestly believing it didn't exist in me at all. We all have parts of us we don't like to acknowledge, but to deny or shame them is to carve off part of us and punish ourselves, which is painful and exhausting. To me, being wholehearted means being able to face, own and re-integrate all parts of ourselves, even the parts we don't like to see. This allows us to let go of the heaviness of that emotional legacy that keeps us half-hearted or closed-hearted and regain its energy. We can then repurpose that energy towards enjoying our lives and towards our vision and the positive difference we want to make in the world for ourselves and those around us.

Once I let go of Scott's fear, I could finally see a positive future for me and even the possibility of bringing a child into the world. So my (now) wife and I planned our family together and I proposed. Within a year, our miracle baby arrived. Surprisingly, I never actually had my vasectomy medically reversed. Once I was ready, life found a way.

In terms of my story, it's very much come full circle. Like my experiences of playing music in groups as a child, my highest highs still come from being a part of a team of people working together. Each person contributing their own part in their own way, but all parts resonating in harmony to create something more powerful than any of us could alone. It's why I invited all the amazing leaders in this book to join and publish together. It paints a far more rich and powerful picture than Rob, my co-facilitator, and I could have produced by ourselves.

And, clearly, Mira agrees. Last night I played some of my favourite music by Jacob Collier through the stereo and we sat and sang along together. I say sang, but in reality I mostly hummed as I didn't know the words, and her singing was more of an atonal cooing, but gorgeous nonetheless. As I hummed, smiling and looking at her laughing and cooing back at me, I was filled with a deep sense of love, joy and connection tinged with a little sadness. A far cry from the emotional numbness I felt at her arrival four months ago. At that stage, I still had work to do on connecting with my emotions. In reality, I still do. We are all complex beings and beautiful works in progress.

I don't usually pay much attention to lyrics, but with impeccable timing in that moment with Mira, Jacob found me:

"In every laugh is the sorrow
Of all of the tears you've held for so long
Would you make me cry?
Oh, let me run dry."

It dawned on me the ultimate payoff we get in life for any experience or achievement is emotions. And although I feel bittersweet about my life and everything that led up to this moment, I wouldn't have it any other way. What an amazing flavour!

I continued singing and smiling at Mira, now with tears rolling down my cheeks. She didn't mind at all. We know we are safe and welcome here. We know we belong.

ABOUT THE AUTHOR
Andrew Ramsden

Andrew Ramsden is an award-winning author, speaker and Sustainable Success Sherpa who has been featured in Business Insider, CEO Weekly and Disrupt Magazine. The Founder and CEO of Peak State Global, Andrew cut his teeth leading large-scale digital and cultural transformation programs in complex organisations. He has since made it his mission to help other executives and leaders reach their peak performance and find sustainable success.

Andrew works with executives and their teams when they're ready to move from fatigued to fulfilled. Having empowered over 7000 leaders from around the world, he has identified the key steps that provide maximum impact with minimal effort. His proven process means they can expand their wealth, connection, time and fulfilment without sacrificing their health.

Andrew is based in Australia with his wife and daughter. When he isn't empowering leaders and their teams he can be found rock climbing or playing drums.

CONNECT WITH ANDREW

Website: *www.andrewramsden.com/revolution*

ROB KIRBY
The Power of Paradox In Performance

In this chapter, I promise to provide you with the essence of the invaluable use of paradox in all areas of performance, including leadership. This includes your business teams, influence on current customers, persuasion of future ideal clients and partnerships, your personal life, mental and physical health, and, most importantly, your relationship with yourself – your own inner being connection.

You will learn that there is always a better way – a more straightforward way – to expand any leader's performance. This begins with an influence that affects everything, including his or her own being. To fully grasp this process, I will thoroughly explain three of the essential paradoxical keys:

1st Paradox – Wholehearted Being vs. Doing

How 'Body Animation' Timelessly Empowers Everything

Your body's ability to position itself to become grounded in the present moment provides you with both awareness and access to the radiance of time in its entirety. This means time in the future, the present moment, and the past are connected to the flesh of our body.

Furthermore, your perception of all phenomena is possible because of the truth of our human body's capacity to experience your unique subjective reality.

Equally mind-blowing, your future and past take up residence within horizons that are revealed in the immediate now because of the animation, position, and posture of your body.

Even more confronting, your birth and death exist entirely in this present moment. All is perceived right now from your position, and the viewpoint you hold about everything is body-energy oriented. You do not need to look beyond yourself. Your essence is a contraction of the whole universe, and it is arranged and laid out before you.

Another important consideration is that your body is the laboratory of life. Your body holds onto defences based on chronic muscle tension/contraction to protect you from more pain or, if you decide to detach from the pain, it allows you freedom from your possible distorted perception of the past, present, and future.

Then, your unimpeded flow of energetic life force (electromagnetic energy) throughout the body allows you to experience the present moment, inclusive of all past moments and future moments integrated as one reality. Remember, you attract what you expect, tolerate, and look for in life based on your body orientation, which holds your core being as closed-hearted, half-hearted, or wholehearted.

The choice is yours. No, you cannot change what happened in your past, but you can effectively change your perception of what happened, thereby authentically building a new *positive positioning* of your past which streams into the present and future.

In the modern world, many people follow gurus or meditation teachers who coach them to live in the moment. This concept is difficult to grasp because this moment is immediately connected to the very recent past and your entire life history and is also connected to multiple generations and forthcoming generations.

Consequently, your future is set in stone – it has already happened because your body holds your perception of reality. So, your future can be seen accurately right now as a struggle or as a complete expansion of everything that you've learned, including your obstacles. This choice becomes an expanded WAY forward, clearly perceived as a great opportunity. This is, of course, because you have the courage to embrace everything – including your darkness.

This moment includes your entire past and your entire future right now and forevermore (including the afterlife). By exploring the above concepts adapted from Dogen, Maurice Merleau-Ponty, and John Pierrakos, you will grasp how your body is the centre of your universe and the cause of your perception of time, space, and all levels of consciousness and all life experience continuously.

Detachment vs. Making it Happen

After experiencing success in both corporate leadership and my personal development business, one of my critical observations is that the biggest blind spot in today's world for both men and women is forcing the outcome of all desires by endlessly trying to 'make it happen'.

The cause of this is taking massive action that is not resonating with your inner being, therefore overriding your wholehearted commitment to your complete truth in business and life. Why? The modern world has become more analytical, and the head is more driven than ever because of the expansion of technology and the motto of 'just do it.'

Accordingly, your body's animation, voice, and posture dynamics with the cosmos are out of sync with the path you've chosen, regardless of whether it is based on seeking security or a path of quick wealth. So many people have left their hearts behind, along with their own spirits.

As an example of this very common form of self-betrayal, I abandoned myself at the turn of the century after having ten years of worldwide success in my new business. I wanted to honour my mentor John, who was 77 years old, and I opened a government-accredited school of Mind-Body Psychotherapy based on character analysis and psycho-dynamic psychotherapy. John evolved his work worldwide for more than half a century, including training for therapists.

My training centre quickly became the largest in the world, and my teacher was very grateful and blown away by the passion of our students. He passed away a year later. The desire to please those we are grateful to often leads to quick decisions that are not embraced by both heart and soul. I was proud that John was grateful and that the school was successful so I could take good care of my family and train competent therapists.

But to open my mentor's school branding, I had to abandon my personal brand, which was growing quickly within several countries. Over the school's ten years, I felt like a headmaster organising worldwide teachers and ensuring students completed their accredited course requirements. My personal brand evaporated and was replaced by the label 'headmaster' – so to speak. That's not me.

I had to then learn detachment. I needed to let go of everything, all 'shoulds' and concepts of doing. I then relinquished and abandoned my pattern of making things happen and doing things constantly to achieve my goal of pleasing someone or proving myself. Why? The why no longer mattered because I was detached.

I first closed the school in 2010 and simply let go. I waited patiently for an organic *inner shift* to be sure my next steps were based on what I loved, so I could embrace the entire universe and expand my body's animation with wholehearted knowledge. I achieved this by embracing and mastering additional modalities and synergistically making the work's evolution my own brand and process.

It was time to fulfil my soul's destiny. By detaching from what I thought I should be doing and allowing my heart and intuition to take over, I stopped forcing and making things happen and followed my heart. I could not have achieved this without guidance from my soul, which guided me to many extraordinary mentors.

Conclusion

The paradoxical balance between being and doing is powerful but requires a capacity to detach from our relentless need to prove ourselves by doing more and more without the balance of deep reflection and self-knowing.

Embracing this paradox will upgrade your performance immediately because it will change your body's animation and dynamic with the entire cosmos and everyone in it, including yourself. Equally important, you will set a great example of a Wholehearted Leader who connects with everyone differently and with the team synergistically without attachments. You will possess the deep humility to embrace a better and more effective way forward, embracing everyone's feedback and identifying/resolving the core obstacle to the business' expanded vision.

2nd Paradox - Change Everything vs. Change the ONE Thing

I was born with haemochromatosis. For most people, it remains dormant for life. But something activated it in me, and my iron levels, specifically the ferritin levels, jumped much higher than normal. My doctor accidentally missed the iron blood work test, so he treated my complex symptoms instead of the root cause:

1. Fatigue…diet changes and more rest
2. Belly fat…diet changes and more exercise
3. Diabetes 2…one script of medication
4. Hypertension…one script of medication
5. Memory loss…one script of medication

For two years, my health was progressively deteriorating, and the side effects of the medications were making the disease even worse. Something within me felt that I had to do something extraordinarily different, or I would lose my grip on life and not be able to do what I loved, which was helping others get to the root cause of their life's challenges. So here was my golden opportunity to walk my talk and diagnose the ONE cause of my illnesses instead of a multitude of symptoms with unnecessary medications.

Accordingly, I went to another doctor, and ONE thing – haemochromatosis was accurately diagnosed as the root cause of all my other symptoms. It consists of a gene called HFE that one inherits from both parents. There is no cure for my disease. My only solution is to donate blood to the Red Cross, or equivalent, every two months for the rest of my life.

The blood donations gradually brought my iron levels back to normal, and there was no longer any need for any medications in my life. Most importantly, my symptoms have slowly vanished, and my energy levels are back to excellent.

I share this story because it is the perfect metaphor for how our modern world tries to impatiently treat symptoms as a quick fix for our physical health, mental health, leadership style, and performance methodology. Also, it is a metaphor for how many people – including very successful ones – lack the ability to get to the root cause of their financial challenges.

Leaders, entrepreneurs, and powerful decision-makers can only become wholehearted when they look at the big picture and observe all dynamics and interactions since everything is connected to everything else. They can then systematically identify and correct the core obstacle or cause that creates an ongoing business crisis with multiple ongoing challenges.

To be perfectly clear, my original doctor was a specialist, very competent and successful, with a longstanding medical career of excellence. He was just *being* a busy human being. We all make mistakes. Some of our mistakes cause large and small businesses to plateau or become obsolete.

That's why business teams that are wholehearted are all teammates because they all want to win and expand, so they cover each other's back. It takes a very committed, high-integrity leader to model this type of performance excellence for the whole team, business, or corporation, which becomes obvious to current clients and prospects.

Conclusion

I believe greatness is built on solid foundations. When you build a launchpad that works effectively over time, the roots have taken hold in the earth. The oldest trees on the planet have grown for centuries. Yes, their roots took hold and bonded with other trees' roots, which strengthened the entire forest.

Simultaneously, as the trees grew, so did their branches. The branches enabled the trees to rise up above the earth and grow continuously over time, all the while remaining loyal to the roots that kept them alive. No roots, no foundations.

No foundation, no growth. No growth, no branches. No branches, no expansion.

Sometimes as leaders, we desire to expand and explore new opportunities. Many business owners seek to branch out and follow what is trending. Just because something is trending does not mean it is better. Often it is contrary to what is better because many people want a quick fix. They lose contact with their own roots and listen to someone who wants to take them in a new direction. Then their foundations start shaking. They lose contact with their own truth. The roots of who they are.

"People turn to spirit when their foundations are shaking; when all along it is spirit shaking their foundations." Dan Millman

The lesson: Stop trying to be all things to all people. Remain loyal to the roots of your foundation, even during the worst times in your life. When you live in truth, people can see the spark in your eye and the authenticity of your body and voice.

When things run amuck, as they sometimes do, just stop. Look for the one cause that has deviated from your core foundation. Then steer your ship back to port while letting go of the symptoms one by one, allowing them to wash away to sea.

3rd Paradox – Build on Character Strengths vs. Transforming

Obstacles One-Focus Process and Diagram

Consider Being and Doing both Concurrently

The depth and power of transformation commence with a bond of truth between me and the client. In other words, we are connected to a shared journey. Neither of us can do this without the other.

This journey begins with One-Focus and remains so throughout the beginning, middle, and end. We reserve the right to commence another shared journey.

The process involves two simultaneous elements designed to bring a profound inner and outer experience of integration of their perception of reality within themselves, thus accelerating their One-Focus outward performance.

These two elements include building performance acceleration on the foundations of your core strengths and simultaneously accessing and transforming your blind spots and obstacles, which become the way forward.

This manifests as a wholehearted lasting experience that has no limitations. The client's potential from the One-Focus Process manifests as an expanded vision and exponentially increases performance excellence. This is built on their working connection with me.

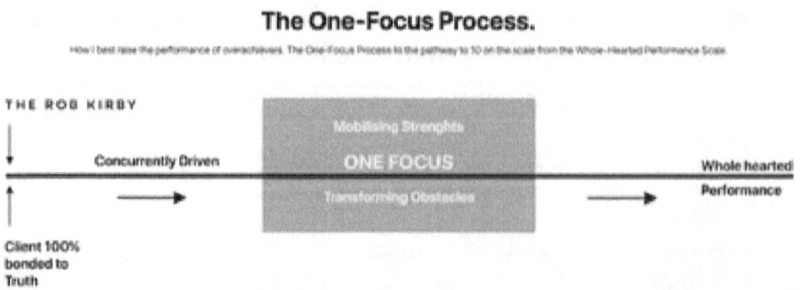

The One-Focus Process.

The reason I facilitate the One-Focus Process on strengths and obstacles simultaneously is that my clients possess two qualities for optimum wholehearted performance, which are necessary for massive brand awareness and business growth:

1. The willingness to take a deep dive way out of their comfort zone to claim what they are best in the world at in their service to humanity.
2. They also possess the humanity to know that their brightest light is eventually dimmed by their own shadow or blind spot, so they know they need a high-level container being held for them to transform darkness into light. I am the holder of their container, light and dark until they fully claim it.

Accordingly, my One-Focus Process becomes their laser beam to become the best version of themselves. They paradoxically keep their eye on the target by mobilising their strengths and concurrently own how their own body-energy system and body's animation to the universe must be transformed into a deeper, stronger, and more powerful version of themselves.

The Speed of Trust

When you live in alignment with your deepest values, people know it. The truth speaks very loudly. Your willingness to speak your truth and consistently communicate to all business associates with transparent vulnerability creates trust like no other approach. If others meet you at this very high vibration, then your mutual success will accelerate at the speed of light. This is my strongest value that I live by and teach to as many people as I can reach in this lifetime.

Conclusion

Where Do You Go From Here to Embrace These Paradoxical Concepts?

In the most recent research from Berkley on entrepreneurs and leaders, they found that 72% reported suffering from mental health issues:

- Depression
- ADHD
- Substance abuse
- Bipolar disorder
- Psycho-somatic illness
- Anxiety-based sleep disorder

Since all symptoms are connected directly or indirectly to your body-mind connection, a lack of awareness of causation typically has a deleterious effect on performance. This is not only subjective but dramatically affected by the entrepreneur's dynamic with me. I allow for rationalisations to be observed but then use these obstacles to expand the entrepreneur's vision and performance. I focus on coaching, mentoring, and mental and physical health with the integration of emotional and social intelligence.

Our modern world treats symptoms (including coaches) without a wholehearted interconnection of all aspects of consciousness, which not only slows down recovery time but diminishes the focus and outcomes of top performers. Drop all excuses and face the truth. It's your life. Effective organic treatment of these issues simultaneously integrates expansion in all areas of life:

Wholehearted Expansion Diagram

The Hero's Journey to Wholehearted Freedom

		Level	State	Attribute
Positive intentions & expectations				High self-esteem
Doesn't take anything personally				Lid-free life/ Low tolerance of disrespect
Momentum		10	Whole-hearted	Faith, 100% certainty
		9	Flow, In The Zone	Know your truth
Self knowledge		8	Fulfilling opportunity	Trust with evidence
		7	Confident expansion	Belief with courage
		6	Strong effort	Positive attitude
Breakthrough	---	---	---	---
		5	Half-hearted	Fear & anxiety
		4	Good effort	Anger & rage
		3	Crisis to crisis	Depression & despair
Empowerment		2	Hanging on	Worry & desperation
		1	Given up / Closed Heart	Terror & numb
Negative intentions & expectations				Low self-esteem
Takes things personally				Lid on life/ High tolerance of disrespect

Conclusion

Personal development worldwide has gone down the path of advocating more and more massive action with a methodology that demands better and better outcomes and mostly bypasses your inner self. Why not do both with equal power? What if your doing was only generated from your divine origins?

Could There Be a Better Way?

Yes, by embracing paradox, leaders can perceive elements of consciousness (which simply means deep awareness) through expansive observation. This will manifest metaphysical insights from a fresh lens that most successful leaders overlook. The result is a performance breakthrough beyond self-imposed limits, which most people – even very successful people – need to be made aware of to catapult them into a state of unlimited expansion. Aside from embracing 'Just Do It' from the Nike ads, I urge you to regularly take time for stillness, observe without judgement, and listen to your heart and intuition.

ABOUT THE AUTHOR
Rob Kirby

Rob Kirby is a world-renowned High-Performance Leadership Guide for entrepreneurs, corporate leaders, and CEOs.

His laser beam focus makes him the best in the world at expanding your greatest strengths everywhere so you can integrate your past, present, and future into right now – you then crack open your most significant obstacle, get the puss out, and merge it into your life's greatest contribution.

He combines advanced degrees in science, business, psychology, and character analysis with decades of learning from the best coaches, trainers, and therapists worldwide. Rob has taken that foundation and combined it with his own highly successful corporate leadership journey and his over 30 years of experience in delivering hands-on and online transformations to the lives, careers, and businesses of tens of thousands of clients from around the world.

Rob treats the root cause of your core issue within the deepest part of your psyche. He possesses insight into what is needed to ignite your greatness towards One thing that is in fact your path of destiny. The result is his proven One-Focus Process developed over three decades to guide clients to unlock their hidden potential and step into their true greatness.

Rob lives in southern California with his son, where he enjoys exercise, meditation, reading, western movies, delicious multicultural food, and his famous superfood smoothies.

CONNECT WITH ROB

Website: *www.therobkirby.com*
Email: *info@therobkirby.com*
Facebook: *www.facebook.com/robert.kirby.710*
LinkedIn: *www.linkedin.com/in/robertkirby-leadership*
Instagram: *www.instagram.com/robertkirby.official*

FEDA ADRA
The Why Behind
Meaningful Connections

I still find it surreal to be referred to as a leader. My personality as a child and for most of my career was someone painfully shy, a trait I considered incompatible with being an effective leader. But I've come to learn that my shyness was a blessing. My parents migrated with their children in the early 70s from Lebanon, a country experiencing war and uncertainty. I was the second youngest of 11 children. I still vividly remember my first day of kindergarten in an unfamiliar country, where I was faced with the daunting experience of fitting into a new environment without knowing a single word of English. It was a scary and lonely experience. From a very young age, I had to help my parents navigate a new language and culture. While this was challenging for me, I picked up the language quickly, and soon found myself acting as the family's unofficial translator. I remember standing in line at the bank with my parents when I was just seven years old. When the person behind the counter asked how he could help, my parents struggled to communicate their needs, because of the language barrier. Without hesitation, my father lifted me up so I could translate for them. Imagine, a little girl trying to talk about money and other adult things, nervously hoping that she was accurately communicating her father's financial requirements.

As I continued to learn and absorb the language, I began to take on more responsibilities as the family translator. I would regularly help my parents fill out forms, read mail, communicate with our neighbours and teachers and translate the nightly news. It wasn't easy, especially since my shyness was often so intense that my face would heat up and become bright red as soon as anybody would start to talk to me. I never felt like I had a real childhood. While others my age would play games with their siblings or friends, I was babysitting my older sister's children. I felt a larger sense of responsibility and I took it very seriously.

Reflecting on my childhood experiences, I understand now how they shaped me into the leader I am today. Being a leader requires a diverse range of skills, including active listening, complex problem-solving, and the willingness to help others in need. It also requires bravery and the willingness to take on challenges. My childhood experiences also had a significant influence on my career choices. I was always drawn to roles where I could use my abilities to help others, which grew into a passion for acts of service and ultimately led me down a career path in the not-for-profit sector.

During my 16-year tenure as CEO of a non-profit organisation, providing community care services for the elderly, I gained a firsthand appreciation for one of the most important leadership skills you can have – creating meaningful connections. One particular project, the expansion of services into a regional town in Queensland, proved to be an enlightening moment for me. We hosted a gathering in a local town hall, to introduce ourselves to the community and talk about our services. During my presentation, an elderly gentleman by the name of Arthur put his hand up and asked to speak. He stood confidently, removed his green cap and looking me in the eye, in his charming Irish accent, posed me a question.

"Can I tell you what it's like to get old?"

After working in the aged care space for 12 years, I thought I had already understood the answer to this question. My work for a long time had been based on assisting elders to maintain their independence as much as possible. But Arthur's answer surprised me.

"Getting old feels like you are disappearing. It is like you are under a rock and nobody ever lifts that rock up to see you." He went on to tell me that his wife had passed away five years ago and how, since her passing, he now rarely saw or spoke to anybody. He was alone and extremely isolated. «And now you are here to save us."

We already provided social support services, but Arthur opened my eyes to the real problem, and its extent. As he spoke, I noticed tears in the eyes of all my staff, as well as my own. His words were incredibly powerful. I had thought I knew how I could help, but I was wrong. There was an epidemic of loneliness and Arthur helped me realise just how important it was to really understand the challenge I was meant to be solving. Without this meaningful connection with Arthur, I would not have had the inspiration to look beyond the services we provide. I knew I had to think more innovatively and that I could not do this alone.

Loneliness for human beings is the cause of many issues, from mental health to physical disease, and our elderly population in particular are really suffering from this. Arthur's courage to tell me what it was really like, and the realisation that followed a few months later, reaffirmed to me the power of creating a safe space for people to speak up and express themselves. It takes courage to speak up and, as a leader, it's crucial to create an environment where people can do so without fear of judgement. But true leadership goes beyond even that. It's about building authentic connections, listening with empathy, and taking action to address the needs and concerns of those you serve. So, I set out to accomplish this and become the type of Wholehearted Leader I knew I needed to be to create change.

As I learned, meaningful connections go beyond simply talking to people. They are about building strong relationships that drive change. In the midst of a busy schedule, I learned a valuable lesson about the importance of being present and involved with my team and clients on a day-to-day basis. One day, while I was rushing through the office to a board meeting, one of our volunteers smiled at me from a distance and waved, as if to try and get my attention.

I remember thinking, *keep walking, keep walking, don't stop, you're late, keep walking, keep walking.*

Despite my best efforts, I succumbed to her endearing smile and, before I knew it, was engaged in the mundane pleasantries of small talk and idle chat. But as we talked, the conversation shifted gears to an 86-year-old client with terminal cancer, who had been looking forward to attending a social event my staff had organised. The volunteer had been driving her to chemotherapy appointments for the past few months and had been told by the client that she only had a few weeks left to live. The volunteer was understandably distressed about the situation. As I listened to her story, I felt a sudden shift in perspective. The board meeting I was late for suddenly seemed utterly trivial and insignificant. I immediately reached out to our team to see what we could do to make this event happen for the client, despite her declining health. We worked quickly to arrange transportation, accommodation, and medical support, to ensure that she and her family could attend the event and make some happy memories in her final weeks.

It's easy to get caught up in the demands of a busy schedule or the pressures of leadership, but our ultimate goal should be to make a positive impact on the lives of others. By taking the time to listen to the stories of others and connect with them on a personal level, we can gain valuable insights and create meaningful change. Through these experiences, I gained a profound understanding of the powerful impact a Wholehearted Leader can have. This is what I learnt:

1. **Get to know the stories of the people around you.** To truly connect with those you lead, it's essential to understand their backgrounds, experiences, and perspectives. Knowing their stories can help build trust and strengthen relationships, creating a more cohesive and collaborative work environment. Ask yourself, do you truly know the stories of the people around you? If you don't know their stories, how can you lead?
2. **Prioritise meaningful connections.** As a leader, it can be easy to get caught up in the demands of a busy schedule or the pressure to perform. Make time for conversations and check-ins and be intentional about building relationships.
3. **Create a safe space.** Creating a safe space for expression is essential for fostering creativity and innovation. When people feel comfortable expressing their thoughts and ideas, they are more likely to develop innovative solutions to problems. By encouraging open communication, you allow people to feel heard and valued, which in turn can inspire them to take on new challenges, take risks and think outside the box.

4. **Use active listening.** This is an essential leadership skill, but it's not something that can be taught in a traditional sense. Instead, it requires a genuine desire to learn about and understand the person you're engaging with, as well as a commitment to being fully present in the moment. Practise curiosity, empathy and being fully engaged and attentive during conversations.
5. **Don't let your position or status get in the way of connecting with others.** As a leader, it's important to lead with humility and empathy. Don't let your position or status create a barrier between you and others. Instead, be approachable, open, and willing to connect with others at all levels of your organisation.

Your Legacy is in Every Meaningful Connection You Make

I've made many meaningful connections over the years. Each holds a special place in my heart and represents the unique relationship I had with each individual. What's interesting about these connections is that they transcend the roles I've had and the companies I've worked with. Whether I was working as a CEO, consultant, or entrepreneur, I've been able to keep these connections with me and many were forged during my most ambitious projects. What's truly inspiring about these connections is that they go beyond simply achieving goals or advancing our careers. They are founded on shared values, mutual respect, genuine care for one another and the greater impact we can make in creating a better world for humanity. It's these deep connections that allow us to collaborate on ambitious projects with passion and purpose, and to push ourselves beyond what we thought was possible.

I've come to learn that smart people like working on solving really complex problems. It was an awe-inspiring realisation that the connections I cultivated throughout my career not only introduced me to remarkable leaders, but also guided me towards my passion projects. To top it all off, one individual I worked closely with on a project ultimately became my employer and business partner. This shows that the bonds we form with others can lead to life-changing opportunities, all of which culminated in the realisation that, while I was good at connecting with others, there was one meaningful connection I had been neglecting.

Forced Stops

My journey towards meaningfully connecting with myself began with a pivotal moment: my first severe anxiety attack and experience with depression. It was a moment of profound suffering. It was just another ordinary weekday morning, and I stuck to my usual routine of waking up bright and early, meditating, and preparing my go-to long black coffee. I cosied up in my favourite armchair, but then something completely unexpected happened. I was hit with an intense wave of nerves that left me paralysed. My hands trembled uncontrollably, and I couldn't make sense of what was going on. To say it was a frightening experience is an understatement and, deep down, I knew that something was seriously wrong. I remember thinking, this cannot be happening right now. I had a full schedule. I was at the end of an important project, working with many collaborators, and my team was relying on me to be well.

I was incredibly fortunate to have the support of my husband, family and medical professionals during this difficult time in my life. I was formally diagnosed with severe anxiety and depression. Despite my career revolving around finding solutions to support others in this area, I had never personally experienced it. I spent the next six weeks getting the help I needed, taking time off and allowing myself to feel the pain. One morning, the overwhelming feeling of fear and anxiety returned as I stood in my kitchen. During this particularly intense panic attack, I had an epiphany. Instead of being consumed by it, I observed my experience. I saw myself, the one suffering and, the minute I became the observer, the anxiety and pain stopped. It was time to listen and understand why it was happening. I felt that this was a strong nudge and a wake-up call to reassess my life.

The Nudge

Resigning was a scary and daunting decision. I had to leave behind my passion projects and the wonderful people I had worked with for so long. But I knew it was time to move on and find where I was truly meant to be. I remember so many people feeling concerned about my decision, and they cautioned me against it. They argued that the projects I was leaving behind were my legacy and I shouldn't abandon them. However, I knew deep down that those projects were not my legacy. In fact, I believe you can never truly know what your legacy is. The impact we make on the lives of others is not always tangible or measurable. You see, every meaningful connection we make throughout our lives has the potential to leave a lasting impact on ourselves and others, and it's impossible to predict the extent of our influence. It's not about leaving behind a particular project or accomplishment that defines us. Although you may never fully know the extent of your legacy, it's important to recognise that its impact is far-reaching and long-lasting.

With no specific role or direction, I took some well-earned time off to ask myself a question: what's next? It was a challenging time, but one that ultimately led me to understand why I burned out and to look at how I could become a better leader.

Connecting with Myself

I now approach my work, my relationships, and my experiences with a new-found sense of clarity and inner peace. It's as if I'm observing everything from a place of deep calm and love. My interactions with loved ones, colleagues, and friends are now infused with a sense of intention, and I am able to lead from a place of meaningful connection with myself first and then with others. While my experience as a child taught me the importance of being brave and helping others, I wasn't taught the importance of self-care and self-love. I never took the time to ask myself what truly motivates me or what I genuinely enjoy doing. The journey towards self-awareness and meaningful connection is not an easy one, but it is one that is deeply worthwhile and rewarding. As I reflected more on my leadership journey and projects, I discovered that the first step to becoming a Wholehearted Leader is to forge a meaningful connection with oneself.

I didn't realise that, even though I loved my work and had many enriching experiences, I was still creating unnecessary suffering for myself and often found myself caught up in the hustle and bustle of it all. This prevented me from fully enjoying the peace and tranquillity that life has to offer. While I achieved incredible business growth and created workplaces where people felt safe and appreciated, it was at the expense of burning myself out and neglecting my own needs and interests. Through my journey towards Wholehearted Leadership, I learned how to work more effortlessly and approach my leadership role with a more relaxed flow. I discovered that a meaningful connection with oneself can provide a foundation for more authentic and effective leadership. My schedule, both professional and personal, is lighter, and my tasks are more intentional, with lots of quiet spaces to read, garden and journal. I wake up every day with enthusiasm for the day and week ahead. When I fall back into old habits of overscheduling, I am aware of what it is doing to my mental health and I reach out for support. I have built a supportive network of individuals, who embrace my strengths and weaknesses and inspire me to think outside the box. You may be wondering if my new approaches have impacted my business results. I'm excited to say that I am achieving more than I ever have and surpassing even my most ambitious goals, in ways I never thought possible.

Connecting with oneself on a deeper level is an essential step towards becoming a successful leader. Balancing the ordinary and the extraordinary in our lives is key to achieving both success and happiness. In my career, I strive to work on the extraordinary, pushing boundaries and achieving new heights. But in my personal life, I find solace in the ordinary, appreciating the simple things that bring me joy and fulfilment.

But how does one do this? This was my journey and I hope that, within it, you may find some tools to support you too:

Practice mindfulness. Mindfulness is the practice of being present and fully engaged in the current moment. By paying attention to your thoughts, feelings, and surroundings, without judgement or attachment, you can develop a deeper understanding of yourself and cultivate inner peace and calm.

Do less. In a culture that celebrates productivity and busyness, it can be easy to fall into the trap of equating success with doing more. However, as I discovered on my own journey towards meaningful connection with myself, this approach can actually be counterproductive. Effortless work is about finding a state of flow, where we are fully immersed in what we're doing and yet not feeling stressed or overwhelmed. It's about letting go of the need to constantly push ourselves to do more.

Engage in self-reflection. Set aside time to reflect on your thoughts, feelings, and experiences. Journaling, meditation, or simply sitting quietly with your thoughts can help you gain clarity and insight into your inner voice. Your inner voice can answer many of the questions you need clarifying.

Cultivate self-compassion. Treat yourself with kindness, empathy, and understanding. Acknowledge your strengths and weaknesses and forgive yourself for mistakes or shortcomings. We are our hardest critics and the story we tell ourselves is sometimes critical. You have the power to reshape the story you tell about yourself.

Engage in activities that bring you joy. Whether it's a hobby, a creative pursuit, or simply spending time in nature, make time for activities that bring you joy and fulfilment. Doing so can help you connect with your passions and your sense of purpose.

Be aware of your suffering – and seek support. Don't be afraid to reach out to friends, family, or a mental health professional, if you need support or guidance on your journey towards self-connection. Remember that meaningful connections with others can also help you deepen your connection with yourself. It's important to feel the pain, as your awareness of it can guide you to address where it is coming from and start the healing process.

Life is a journey filled with experiences that shape and mould us into who we are today. Our childhood experiences, our interactions with the world around us, and our personal journeys all play a vital role in shaping our perspectives and attitudes. Regardless of your role or your feelings towards your work, it's important to take ownership of your future and break the cycle of busyness. You don't have to wait for a negative situation or external event to give you the push you need to make changes. Remember, the power to shape your future is in your hands. Don't wait for others to make things happen for you; be your own nudge and take action today. Embrace the abundance that life has to offer and create a future that is truly your own. I encourage you to begin your personal journey of self-discovery and connection. Acknowledge and learn from your life experiences. And remember that connecting with oneself is a lifelong journey; one that requires patience, dedication, and self-compassion.

ABOUT THE AUTHOR
Feda Adra

Feda Adra is an inspiring business and industry leader, renowned for her entrepreneurial mindset and unwavering commitment to achieving 'the greater good' Feda has consistently demonstrated her innovative approach to community care, leading organisations through extraordinary growth and initiatives that drive positive change.

At the heart of Feda's leadership success lies her ability to connect, influence, and inspire. She has a compelling vision and foresight, as well as the courage to challenge the status quo to empower her team to embrace change and cultivate creativity through an entrepreneurial culture grounded with the core values of 'doing and being more'.

A passionate collaborator, Feda has established strong industry and cross-sector connections, fostering collaboration to find game-changing services and products that improve the health and well-being of communities.

Feda has been a resident of Sunshine Coast in Queensland, Australia, since 1995, where she lives with her husband and has raised three children. Over the past 25 years, Feda has led purpose-driven organisations supporting youth, aged care, disability, and mental health services. Her leadership and achievements have been recognised with several business leadership awards across her career.

Outside of her work, Feda is a dedicated gardener and nature enthusiast, finding inspiration in the natural environment. She believes that mindfulness and time spent in nature can help people tap into their inner wisdom.

CONNECT WITH FEDA

Website: *www.wearespur.com*
LinkedIn: *www.linkedin.com/in/feda-adra*

DAVID BEAL
The Art Of Doing Nothing

Over the last 37 years, I have been fortunate to have had opportunities to develop many high-performing teams in many different contexts covering education, finance, government, profit for purpose and community groups. Many of the leaders I have been blessed to have played a role in developing have gone on to develop other leaders at senior levels. One of whom has brought together this amazing group of people to write this highly relevant and useful tool for a leader to have in their tool kit.

Authentic, wholehearted, and whole-of-person leadership is an art form that one enjoyably spends their life refining and improving. It requires you to be honest about your true intent and your own ego and it demands a commitment to self and others. The joy of seeing others reach their potential is rewarding and challenging. I would suggest, however, that it is not hard if you have a solid tool kit and know your own weaknesses and strengths.

Not Doing Anything

I would like to share some methods and tactics I put loosely into the 'Do nothing' category. Granted, deliberately doing and saying nothing could be viewed as doing something. But for the sake of agreement, let's call doing nothing just that. There is a plethora of information on what to do in different situations to develop your leaders. My 'Do nothing' category is underpinned by the premise that you yourself must be prepared to hand over and let go (pass the baton, relinquish control/accountability/responsibility, etc.). This can apply to big things or small things. It can be handing over the responsibility of a group of divers to your dive master while you assist a new diver or handing over responsibility for getting all the items needed for a Joeys' sewing badge night. Handing things over can be a challenge for us for a lot of reasons and it is the subject of many disciplines and research. Two principles I employ at different times to help me hand over are:

- Work Yourself Out of a Job
- Embrace the Dignity of Risk

The following examples and situations incorporate these two principles and begin to explore them.

By sharing the three 'Do nothing' examples below, I hope to provide you with some strategies and tactics that you can use to continue to develop your emerging leaders and grow in your own journey as a leader.

During my time as Group Leader of the West Centenary Scout Group, I learnt quickly that there is usually always someone that has an opinion that the way you did things could have been better. This can be done with no malintent, or it can be highly pointed. Situation resilience as a leader is crucial. Often these people, as it turns out, can excel in doing a better job. And that is perfect when you've already given 26 hours in the day, haven't had dinner yet and really need someone, anyone, to help out. So, the challenge I faced was finding methods to hand over responsibility to them.

As the Group Leader, I was responsible for three dens, 150-plus youths (from Joeys to Rovers), 20 volunteer leaders and 30 active parent helpers. I was also required to manage the parents/carers of the 150-plus youths. I was also at the time the Venture Leader and had been a cub and scout leader as well as the Quartermaster. Working in an environment that is run purely on a volunteer basis brings about a range of challenges that are not present in an environment where one is paid to perform. People who volunteer are typically involved because they believe in the cause, not because of skill or merit. They may have that, but that is not the primary credential for participation.

I have to paint a picture of what it's like in these kinds of organisations when going on a three-day camp in tents in the bush with 30 youths aged from 7 to 11. There is usually a core group of registered leaders — two. And, if you're lucky, two or three willing adults jump in and help. But there are plenty of adults dropping off their children and asking what time they need to pick them up in two days' time. Or asking if [name] could be dropped back a bit earlier. It's a daunting and rewarding challenge. On the return and handover of their wonderfully behaved and innocent child, there would more often than not be the critical and considered feedback you've been looking forward to.

One of the methods for handing over responsibility I found highly useful and successful was totally ignoring certain situations until someone did something about it. One of the first times I deployed the 'ignore a problem and do nothing' approach was related to a sewing badge night we had for the Joeys one evening. There was a particular parent that seemed to thrive on educating me on how things could be planned better. Despite many attempts to encourage them to help out, they remained on the sideline. Their child was going to participate in the activity and there was concern about what was required for the evening: Where was the material coming from? Who had the patterns, etc.? I decided to hold off on responding until the last possible point before it was really too late. Sure enough, a few days into the silence came the "Sorry but I've spoken to a few other parents and, well, I organised for some material and patterns from a friend. Someone is bringing pins and scissors, etc." email.

Yes, that came with post 'sewing badge success' comments of 'poor leadership' or 'lack of attention.' But that is not relevant if you don't take that on board or get caught in the often never-ending cycle of justification and explanation, during which many people's ability to clearly communicate is diluted with emotion.

A simple "Thanks so much for doing that. You did a great job, by the way. I was thinking about the next activity and if we have time for it or not" can turn a situation around. Offering thanks, a compliment, and a potential new thing to solve redirects many a personality. This individual jumped straight to the next challenge and went on to become a Joey leader and work with other parents to participate more.

Selecting when to do nothing and ignore something requires careful consideration of the situation, the capability of the individual and the safety of others. As a leader of emerging leaders, we have a great responsibility, and we must not forget that our actions can grow people but they can also hinder and hold back.

Work Yourself Out of a Job

I think it is fair to say that many of you will have met leaders that really need to move on. Staying in a leadership role beyond your time can be damaging to a team and your emerging leaders. It can hinder progress, reduce innovation and stifle new ideas. It does this to the team, the business and often yourself.

Recognising when your time is up is a complex and challenging journey. The role of mentoring and guiding in the early stages of the journey is recommended. This can be informal or formal, but it is a must in each new leader's journey.

Walking alongside individuals to support them to become what they can be is a privilege and an honour. It is also very much part of being a Wholehearted Leader. Our job as passionate, sincere and heartfelt leaders will be limited if we stay too long in one spot. Growth as an emerging leader within many teams and business units across the globe is dependent on an existing leader's role becoming vacant. That means our pool of leaders to develop can be restricted as well.

"Work yourself out of a job" sort of sounds counterintuitive, doesn't it? I am often met with a cocked head and raised eyebrows when I mention this concept. "What do you mean 'work yourself out of this job?' You just got here." I have for many years advocated and worked on the principle that if I work myself out of a job or work myself into a position where I'm not needed any longer because I've developed people who can replace me and take my role, I become more valuable to the organisation.

I become free to pick up new challenges or to be utilised in different ways as required by the organisation. If I create a dependency on myself, not only do I cut off opportunities for myself, but I also hinder people within my team from growing and advancing. Why is that important? Many people think that having a team rotating its leaders may bring instability or slow down momentum in outcomes and benefits realisation. New leaders bringing different ideas and directions can often slow projects and change their scope or vision. If you have developed a solid vision that can be contributed to or improved on and that is truly owned by other people, then keeping the leadership within the team is positive fuel for momentum and continuation as well as speed to market and innovation.

You have set a vision, built a team and are enjoying success. You have capable people and solid leaders that you have developed. Everyone knows your approach to moving on at some point. Don't let thoughts like It will fall apart without me or It's my baby or They are not ready or It's who I am hold you back from your own growth and opening another door and chapter to your life. Be bold and true to yourself when you sense it is time to move. The 'work yourself out of a job' approach sets an expectation within your teams that it's okay to move on, that by ensuring the people in your team are developing others who can take over their roles they are freeing themselves up for new challenges and other opportunities. It continues down the chain.

It also contributes to achieving shared success and ownership within the environment. Having the mindset that you want to work yourself out of your role and replace yourself is a way of demonstrating wholeheartedness and the belief you have in the people you've been developing and leading. It shows people that you believe they can do what you've both been working towards.

You can become irrelevant because they are ready to carry the mantle.

This mindset also contributes to other tactics, such as doing or saying nothing or removing yourself from certain meetings and decision-making processes with comfort and confidence. It gives us the right intent from the beginning of developing others — that intent being handing over things we do to others so they can grow, even if that means a loss of some activity we enjoy. People need experience in order to solidify their learnings. If you keep doing the things that others need to experience, how will they experience them? Handing over accountability and/or responsibility to others does not need to be a major life event worthy of a local news broadcast. It can be as simple as handing off the role of Chair to a project board to one of your leaders. It can be handing over decision-making to someone at a meeting as your representative.

It can be a scary thing as a leader to hand over the mantle to the leaders you've been developing.

Often as leaders we find a value proposition that, to a varying depth, is grounded in what we are bringing other people, the vision we have led the development of, the executive meetings and conversations or the public speaking and events. If we move on to other opportunities, we can wonder if we can do the same again. *Can I repeat what I have done here?* I can assure you that there is not a successful leader who has not asked themselves questions like that. I dare say that question holds many people back in many different situations.

For anyone who is sensing it's time to move on but is held back by these sorts of thoughts, I have used this approach for many years in my professional life. This approach has given me the freedom to take up a vast array of opportunities. The outcomes of many past projects and achievements are still in place today. I started a public service position as an A06 (mid-level officer) and became the Chief Transformation Officer of a large Disability Support organisation within 13 years; experiencing Director and General Manager roles on the way, while finishing a master's degree at the age of 42. I encourage you to be true to yourself and your own journey and hand over the mantle if you're sensing it's time.

If this is the first time you've had to decide to move on, then I assure you the joy and value you feel now will come again. Your next team will be different, and it will not be the same.

As someone who repeated Year 11, had to have remedial, after-school education through high school, was diagnosed with high-level dyslexia, had to wear an external head brace to adjust my teeth during school and was a common target of schoolyard bullies, I understand that we have barriers that can hold us back. From experience I can say with confidence that they diminish in relevance the less focus we give them. And they can become an asset in our journey. They help our empathy level for others. They give us connection points if we are open about them. Very little is unsurmountable with the right intent, mindset and toolkit.

Silence as a Nudge/Push

I am never surprised by the number of times I have seen a person who is ready to step up but is just not doing so. We often find ourselves seeing that people are ready well before they themselves see it or, in some cases, accept it. Offering an opportunity to take the next step can be refused regardless of the eloquence of your approach or argument if the person does not yet have belief and confidence. A gentle nudge or push is sometimes required to generate that belief and confidence.

One of the most successful tactics I have used to help give people a safe and gentle push is to say nothing at specific times and situations. That opens a door for someone to step into. Often without them having any pre-thought or time for any negative thoughts, doors that have been left ajar for someone can open up further. I found over time that people in this situation more often than not kick into gear and surprise themselves. This act of not saying anything also includes not being around or present.

Fear, as we know, is an incredibly powerful force that can hold us back and inhibit growth, hiding with relative ease, depending on the strength we give it, and our belief and self-confidence. Fear can often hold people back from stepping into the role that you've been helping them grow into and to take on. It can seem daunting to a new leader as they step into a role and become that key point in a team. Carrying the responsibility and outcome of a decision that may go wrong can be scary. Overthinking situations and perceived outcomes of a possible mistake, getting something wrong, making a mistake and just generally not getting it right is part of learning. We must reinforce this regularly to others as well as ourselves.

Dignity of Risk

I came across the concept of Dignity of Risk while undertaking Disability studies. For me, it has been one of these things you find in your life that stick with you and you reuse. I summarise the concept as allowing people to make informed choices and decisions, even if it's not what we would do ourselves. I believe that it's important for our emerging leaders to fail safely, and to learn from that in a positive and growth mindset way. Dignity of Risk guides people who play a support role for a person with a disability to ensure that the individual being supported is always able to decide on something, even if everyone around them knows that success is not likely. It is the right to be able to fail and learn in a safe environment. The use of this principle has enabled me to be at peace with any concerns or worries I have about one of my emerging leaders failing or making a mistake. It is up to us to find the right time and situation to enable safety in failure.

Understanding that enabled me to be comfortable randomly putting people on the spot as a nudge or push mechanism. Putting someone on the spot does not have to be an overt and uncomfortable thing. It can be as simple as the sound of silence or not saying anything or being suddenly absent at selected moments.

You might have been developing someone within your team to step into a leadership role and they are still hesitant, you can see it in them and you can see that they're ready, but they can't. This again is where the power of saying nothing at the right time can act as that little push, that gentle little bit of encouragement for people to step into what they are capable of.

Let's say you've been working on securing a deal with a vendor that rests on an important point yet to be agreed. You've been mentoring and leading someone who is ready to start leading future negotiations but is still not participating at key points during the current meetings. They are familiar with the situation, and they know the importance of the final aspect of the deal.

You're in the final meeting and the vendor has neglected to bring up the important point. You're aware of that and can see that your emerging leader is waiting for you to bring it up. This is a good opportunity to just hold back and wait for the last possible moment to give them a chance to jump in. I have found that more often than not, people do jump in. Occasionally you need to give approval in the form of a "Anything I have missed?" directed at them.

This tactic also works in those meetings where a decision is required, and a differing of opinion exists. Depending on the importance of the decision, hand it over to your emerging leader. Don't make the decision; instead say something like, "That's up to you to decide. I'll support your decision." This can be used for small or major decisions depending on where the person is in their growth.

I regularly use this approach as I start to introduce decision-making outside of what an emerging leader's typical remit is. It's part of the 'work yourself out of a job' approach and intent. You're always looking for opportunities to hand over and extend someone into your own territory. You're constantly looking to hand over aspects of your own job to your leaders. And you're teaching them to do the same. Can you see how this can develop into a cycle of growth and Wholehearted Leadership — developing and cementing a leadership-focused culture in an organisation?

Another 'do nothing' tactic is to suddenly have something you need to address at the same time as a meeting that your emerging leader is going to be attending. To be clear, I am not advocating lying or making something up. That would not be genuine. As a senior leader, one always has an outstanding task list of things that need to be done. All I am suggesting is that you prioritise one of them over attending a regular meeting. Once you have chaired or played a key role in several project boards, working parties, task forces, etc., you forget the joy and sense of importance/value that comes when you first start attending and running them. We must be mindful that for us as seasoned leaders and professionals we have grown used to many things that for others are still a big deal. What we have experienced in our journey our emerging leaders are not likely to have done so yet. The things that we do now out of instinct because we have done them so many times does not apply to new leaders. Don't underestimate what something like running a meeting, albeit for one session, means to a new leader. It can be a big deal for them. It is likely to be the topic of conversation after work the first time someone does.

Suddenly not being available for a meeting and asking your emerging leader to jump in and run it until you get there can be a useful and deliberate nudge. What defines 'suddenly' is usually dependent on the person and the situation. It can range from a few hours' notice to five minutes before it starts.

As with all things in leading and managing people, the timing and approach must be done with consideration of the person you're developing — their learning style, personality, background, reliance levels, what's going on in their personal life, etc.

The times I have had the most success with this tactic have been:

- They have an agenda item or a presentation planned, and will have prepared and been ready mentally for that anyway. And you know they are ready for that because you've been leading and developing them in that preparation as a professional.
- The agenda is light, and no discussions are likely to occur that you don't think the individual is ready for. This assumes the individual has been part of the meetings previously and is aware of the flow and structure. They are really there to step through the agenda. This works well for individuals who are good with structure and hierarchy.
- To show an individual they are not ready to run a meeting and it is safe to do so without damaging the individual's progress: safe failure. This goes back to the principle of Dignity of Risk, the right to learn. That is why as leaders and developers of people we must be able to identify and understand our emerging leaders' learning and response styles, working alongside them to understand their preferred styles and when to use other styles as required.
- To increase the branding of an emerging leader. The use of the 'I have to attend to something else so [name] is going to run the meeting this morning' to a senior stakeholder in the meeting whom you're wanting to show the potential of [name]. Letting the emerging leader know what you're doing in this scenario is dependent on what is best for that individual.

It would be remiss of me not to discuss the role and use of body language as a type of silent nudge or push. Body language as a leading and lagging communication tool is well studied and researched. It is without a doubt one of the top tools you can have in your kit. I would go as far as saying that a solid understanding and use of body language is a core fundamental skill to successful leadership and leadership development.

If you have just begun developing your skills in this area, a good place to start is in the use of an open, palm-up hand gesture to point to your emerging leader during a meeting when you are asked a question that you want the person to step up and own. The power of an open-palm hand gesture pointed to someone else in redirecting with authority and confidence cannot be underestimated. It makes a public statement of handing over and gives support and belief in your emerging leader.

I hope that it is obvious to say that you do not do this to pass blame or infer that it is someone else's fault. As I have said a few times, care must be taken with all the approaches you implement with individuals. Being accountable and responsible for their growth and journey is an honour that requires us to consider the whole person and have the right intent to be genuine and wholehearted. If more of us do this, imagine what sort of transformation or revolution could take place in workplace and community leadership.

ABOUT THE AUTHOR
David Beal

David is an award-winning leader with over 37 years of experience in developing teams and leaders across education, finance, local and federal governments, profit for purpose and Community Group environments. He uses his demonstrable and evidenced-backed growth mindset to walk alongside others and deliver major projects and reforms. He has been accountable for many State Government election commitments and has taken part in several Royal Commissions. His teams have won awards for Courage and Integrity, Innovation and Agile Project management. As a leader of leaders, David uses his vast expertise and belief in a whole-person approach to leadership to partner with people to help them realise their potential. His accountabilities at an Executive level cover Portfolio and Program Management, Data and Information management, Application development, ICT, Cyber Security, User Centred Design and Experience and Board level Strategy development. He is currently the Chief Transformation Officer for a large disability organisation and a Senior Advisor for a boutique Australian ICT and digital advisory company.

CONNECT WITH DAVID

LinkedIn: *www.linkedin.com/in/dbeal*

CHERYL CRUTTENDEN
Be Out Standing In Your Field

As I sit here writing this chapter, the call to prayer rings out. This is the soundscape that is Marrakesh. This one mysterious voice rises above the busyness of everyday life, way above the din of the Medina and Djemaa El Fna, with its cacophony of drummers and snake charmers playing their high-pitched trumpeting horns, their snakes lazily raising their heads, not really interested in striking anything … the traditionally dressed dancers in their vibrantly coloured Moroccan robes of blues and reds, spinning, clapping and swirling their tasselled caps to the accompaniment of more and louder drums, horns and cymbals that pierce the ears. I wonder if they love doing this dancing as a form of expression, or is it simply a means to an end?

There's the solo musician, seemingly multi-armed, playing a long, horn-like instrument, while also playing a keyboard, drumming and singing into a microphone, all amplified and slightly distorted; men with monkeys, one in a dress, one in shorts, one wearing a nappy, either sitting on small pedestals, gazing with eyes fixed on their handler awaiting their next performance instruction to flip, or pulling at the ends of their chains before being placed on the shoulder of a tourist for a photo, also accompanied by loud drummers and horns; the ladies calling out, plaiting hair and applying henna tattoos; vibrant stalls layered with a multitude of beautifully coloured fresh fruits for juicing; the myriad of leather, brass, slippers, shoes, argan oil, spices, sunglasses, hats and assorted clothes stalls; and the street food vendors and eateries with spruikers encouraging you to eat there, all with the happy promise of good food and no gastro. It is a sea of movement and colour, all competing for the attention of the visiting traveller, in exchange for goods, a couple of photos and a few coins in their hat, day after day after day.

There are crowds of people all rushing somewhere and then there are the raggedly clothed bodies begging, sitting or lying on the sidewalk, amid the army of legs marching by, largely ignored by locals and tourists alike.

And the cars and motorbikes— oh, the motorbikes! With a mix of healthy to unhealthy banging, rattling engines and loud exhausts … young men hooting along, holding up their phones in front of them, women wearing dresses billowing out behind them, and just there, the one-legged bearded man on a noisy ancient motorbike, his crutches strapped along the foot pedals, using a hand lever to shift gears as he roars by.

And then— oh, my heart—lined up in rows there are easily over a hundred pairs of horses, harnessed up to beautifully coloured, shining carriages. Some are in good condition, many are not. I try not to be judgemental but with a horse woman's eye I find myself looking at the condition and trim of their shod hooves, sores from ill-fitting harnesses and being nipped by others, some that limp as they trot by on the hard roads, others pawing at the ground, heads tossing and stomping hooves shaking off the hundreds of flies, standing for hours without eating, the dropped heads and sullen looks of some, while others lay their ears back and with teeth bared, threaten to bite as you walk by.

The human body is simply not designed for such a relentless assault on the senses and nervous system. The continuous cacophony of sounds, colour and movement suddenly seems to get overwhelmingly louder. The heat, the smells, the crush of waves of bodies … as I try to cross a road with bikes and carts heading towards me from all directions, seeming to grow exponentially as I begin to focus more and more on what I perceive to be the negative aspects of things. Then the judgemental self-talk begins.

There's suffering here. Tourism can be such a blessing and a curse. Many of these people and animals would not be here if not for people like me visiting.

Then this hauntingly beautiful call arises and floats out from the minarets, across the rooftops, pure and untouched by the cacophony of sounds that continuously emanate from the marketplace below.

The muezzin calling the faithful to prayer from the main mosque, the Koutoubia Mosque. Its minaret has been standing guard over the old city since the Almohads erected it in the 12th century.

For me, it too is a call. A call to awareness. Something that I never used to do, until I began this work. Looking again at the horses, I'm reminded that perhaps this is their greatest lesson for me. This is one of their special gifts: full body presence, awareness, without judgement or story.

Here lies my choice point: to allow the environment to impact my thoughts, emotions and behaviour and go down the road I used to, focusing on the negative and all that I could find wrong or cruel, being reactive and creating and adding story that continues to activate my nervous system, thus taking me out of relationship with myself and others.

Or, by paying attention to my intention, take action to befriend my nervous system for self-care. I can notice my internal felt senses but if this is too overwhelming or I'm in a high-stakes environment, instead I can direct my attention to focus on the external, on the positive, to what brings me joy.

I quickly check in. *What is driving me? Am I leading my life or is life leading me? Where's my attention, my focus? What am I experiencing, thinking, feeling? What is the story I'm making up? Is it serving and resourcing me in this moment or not? What do I want to have happen, to experience? What do I need to do for self-care?*

I begin to breathe a little easier in that moment of stopping and feeling, noticing the colour and texture of the purple bougainvillea flowers; the long, flowing jet-black mane on one of the horses; the beautiful indigo-blue kaftan with intricate gold embroidery on the person walking past; the rhythmic regulating sound of horseshoes on pavement, and I feel my nervous system settle as I consciously direct my attention, using all of my senses to experience the moment. Letting go of judgement that what I'm seeing and experiencing should somehow be different. Amid the busyness, an ease emerges as I reconnect with myself, to what has heart and meaning, even amongst all this noise and distraction.

Some may dislike the call and label it noise pollution and, yes, if you focus on the quality of the loudspeakers, they do detract somewhat from the beauty of it. Yet I find it soothing to the soul, a reminder to experience peace and serenity amongst the din of daily life.

I love the sound of this prayer as it reverberates across the rooftops and land. It's not the same when listening to a recording of it. There's something deeply evocative that arises in one's core when you hear it 'live' and allow it in. For me, it possesses a mysterious, attractive force that is not just about being in a foreign country. It's not the head-based knowing that "you're not in Kansas (or Australia!) anymore, Dorothy."

It's a visceral body-based response and it brings tears to my eyes when I allow my body to resonate with this ancient call, or indeed other chants or tones.

The call to prayer (adhan) is delivered five times a day, chanted by a muadhin, who is chosen for his voice and singing skills, to remind Muslims to come to mandatory prayer and to leave worldly matters behind. I love the nature-based connection with the timing also, being fixed by daily astronomical phenomena, related to the solar diurnal motion, which varies with latitude and longitude.

I've heard that this call is a precursor to telecommunication. It is a means of communicating to people across great distances, as each mosque sends out their own call, adding to, linking up, contributing to the spread of the call, connecting all in the same moments across the land. I wonder if there must be some sort of field effect, a resonance that emerges in connecting.

With the rise of mindfulness practices, many people are now doing similar. Setting the call 'to announce or inform' via a phone or watch. A reminder to give themselves time, several moments a day, to also switch off, disconnect from their busy work schedule and spend time in a practice connecting to self. Maybe to breathe consciously and let go of a little stress, maybe even experience a moment of gratitude.

What's ironic is that this mindful moment is often goal-oriented. It used to be for me too. It was just another goal to be ticked off the day's list, done from a head-based doing perspective, rather than from heart-based being or feeling.

I used to be this person. Endless head-based lists of objectives and goals to be achieved, driven by the gut-based needs of safety, survival and identity. I learnt to swim almost before I could walk and swam competitively until 18 years of age. Winning provided a sense of achievement, and identity. I also rode horses competitively until my early twenties, along with many years of engaging in and leading groups in a range of outdoor adventure activities—bushwalking, hiking, overseas travel, rock climbing, cycling and kayaking. All individual activities and all goal based. Higher, faster, more rugged, more destinations, longer distances and the like were goals that would never end, adding to the sense of who I thought I was. And because they were individual activities, I didn't need to rely on anyone else; I alone was responsible for my success or failure. It was years later I realised that I had no one to commiserate with. I also had no one to share the joy and celebration as a team member with either.

Several years ago I discovered that this constant need for doing, for busyness and achievement, along with the stimulation of being somewhere new and exciting, is actually a trauma response. I used to be so proud of my ability to keep going. Just don't slow down, and never, ever stop, you might actually feel something. Escaping into doing was a great way to keep myself emotionally numb.

I'd constantly drive and push myself to eat less, get fitter, and work through pain and injuries. I once raced in an important swimming competition with a broken wrist (told myself it was just a little sore), hiked for three days over rugged coastal terrain carrying a heavy backpack with a seriously sprained ankle (hell, I'm leading a group hiking for five days, I can't just stop) and cross-country skied for two days with a bruised, severely sprained finger that, 30 years later, still gives me grief. I ignored my body so much that it eventually stopped communicating with me altogether. It has taken some time simply to re-establish these neural networks and retrain my nervous system.

Don't misunderstand me, the creative head brain is a wondrous, amazing thing—just look at what mankind has invented. However, issues arise when this creativity is driven solely by the gut and its need for safety, survival, identity. When this happens, the desires of the compassionate heart are rarely taken into consideration.

Being social animals, and with their huge hearts and guts, horses are great partners for helping in this reconnecting. Their entire body is a sensory information system, which has largely been conditioned out of us. Through their responses, we learn how we unconsciously show up in relationship with ourselves and with others.

This is particularly important in these high-stakes times of rapidly increasingly complex, volatile and often emotional social and business environments.

Few people realise how contagious emotions are. Without awareness, self- and co-regulation, they can spread through our herds, our families, our organisations and our communities like wildfire.

Like horses, being animals, our body contains a distributed intelligence that can be tapped into. Leaders who can access this, especially the head, heart and gut brains, and harness this full intuitive and innate intelligence, are at a distinct advantage.

Just like approaches to horse training and horsemanship has evolved over the years, a new form of organisational leadership is required. Not simply a new approach or model—it's deeper than that; it's about the leader themselves and their ability to develop new levels of consciousness and wisdom in the decision-making process.

Adaptive and generative leadership skills are required now more than ever, and this requires new ways of thinking, feeling, being and doing because any strategies developed and executed from the past, through outdated conditioned ways of being and thinking (which are often informed from maintaining one's identity, status or gut-based survival energy), simply end up back in the old status quo.

The difference is that when we communicate with, align and integrate our conscious and unconscious intuitive abilities, we are able to harness the innate wisdom of the creative head, the compassionate heart and the courageous gut intelligences. Considering these multiple points of view and gathering more information naturally makes for more powerful, wise and generative decision-making.

Even now, sitting on this lounge on a beautifully tiled rooftop of a Riad in Marrakech, with the warmth of the sun on my back and the calming sounds of water trickling into the pool below, I can feel this tug. This pull of the head to stop wasting time sitting here and just get out there and tick off that sightseeing list. Any distracting movement would be better than to sit here mindfully with my thoughts and history. Just thinking about this two-way pull, I feel the tension arise in my body, my shoulders lift, my hands tighten, my breath rises and becomes shallower.

So what changed?

Silent, seated meditation never really worked for me; I never became any more Zen-like. Years of tai chi helped, as I loved the movement aspect, yet I was still caught up in doing. Doing and achieving, looking to advance to the next level or the next form to be mastered without any real deep and lasting satisfaction.

I thought I was being in my doing, and the breathing aspect was powerful for settling the body/mind system, but I was still mainly doing. Still thinking it, more than feeling or being it.

I'd read a book years ago called *Spontaneous Evolution* by Bruce Lipton, in which he writes about the evolutionary process not always taking millions of years, that healing or shifts can occur quickly and spontaneously. This I feel is what I experienced. This was my light bulb moment, my 'aha', my epiphany, and it involved a horse.

A horse? Yes.

What words arise for you when you think and feel into the archetypal qualities of Horse?

List them now. Go on. No, really, do it. Make a list, even just a few words. I'll wait.

Now you've made a list, reflect on each word, one at a time. Close your eyes and feel into the word. Don't think about the word, FEEL the word through your body.

As you feel the word, what do you notice? Where does your attention go in your body?

What shifts in your awareness and body as you begin to 'be' and experience the quality of that word a little more?

What felt sensations arise?

Notice any changes or shifts in one or more aspects: your overall posture; thoughts or images; breathing rate and quality; your felt sensations ... anything?

Perhaps some words that arose for you when reflecting on these qualities were: power, freedom, nobility, vulnerability, strength, courage, community, independence, compassion, herd or relating: empathy, gentleness, speed, agility, intuition, passion.

It's interesting that these are also sought-after qualities of great and impactful leaders, teachers, parents, or any profession that involves interacting with other people.

So why don't some of us feel and why do we need to feel more? Well, everything we encounter in life creates sense and sensation in and through our body. Many people are conditioned out of feeling and developmental experiences or trauma can also create a disconnect. It's just too overwhelming or uncomfortable to feel.

Yet we can't actually choose to feel only the so-called positive emotions and close off the negative. When we shut down feeling, all are shut off and the body stops communicating with us.

Growing up, we learn through experience and our body and physiology impact our thoughts. Every thought, every movement, every breath, every image that arises in our mind's eye, the body registers and shares with us through the felt senses and nervous system functioning. We can't really and truly embody many crucial leadership qualities if we've cut parts of ourselves off. Qualities such as empathy, compassion, creativity and courage can only be fully expressed, and felt by others, when allowed and deeply felt through the body. Otherwise they remain a purely head-based concept.

This is part of the power of working with horses. Being preyed upon by other animals, horses are intuitively tuned to and respond to any shifts in their environment, including the energy and intention of beings around them. They can read us like a book and respond to how we show up, our energetic signature if you like—aspects such as our posture, the rate and quality of our breathing, heart rate variability, emotions, temperature, whether we are conscious of this or not. And they do it all without bias or judgement of right or wrong. You might be able to fake it with others, but you never can with a horse.

Even feeling nothing is still something. So if you said, "Nahhh, nothing came up for me" in that little exploration we did, you still experienced something. So, what does nothing feel like? Be gentle with yourself. If you are like me, after years of being disconnected from your body's intelligence, it can take some time to get the re-communication happening, but like the head brain, the heart and gut intelligence has neuroplasticity also and through attention and intention, we can begin to rebuild those neural networks.

Researchers have discovered that both the heart and gut are involved in the processing and decoding of 'intuitive information'. With the huge heart and gut-brain of Horse, it's no wonder they are such helpful guides to awareness. Studies show that the heart appears to receive intuitive information before the head brain does. Maybe that's why we have the saying, "Follow your heart and you will never go wrong."

Thus, being wholehearted is an integral part of the intuitive process. It has its own intelligence, enabling it to act independently, learn, remember, and generate feelings and certain hormones. The heart's electromagnetic signals not only affect our own behaviour but can also be sensed by the people and animals around us.

This head/heart/gut interaction and intuiting ways of knowing is also well-known in ancient wisdom practices. Enhancing intuition and non-local ways of knowing—that gut feel—are also core to wisdom in leadership.

Our minds only truly know what our bodies have shared with us and this, of course, is highly filtered through our conditioning and experiences. Play with the word exercise some more—choose another word; be curious and notice what stays the same or changes. The more you feel and embody the qualities you desire, the more those neural networks grow and the wiser you become.

So what was my 'aha' moment, my lessons from Horse?

I grew up with horses, hanging out with them, but back then it was mainly about having fun and goals, riding, competing, training, doing.

It wasn't until I discovered that there was a field of practice that combined my two greatest loves, human development and horses, as a form of experiential learning and coaching, that I really began to tap into my heart to lead my life and take gutsy action, rather than life leading me.

It was the final exercise, day six of a training in learning how to facilitate this work with six horses. It had been an intensely hot and dry summer of disastrous bushfires.

Everyone was hot and tired, including the horses, I suspect, as they were simply standing around. We were inside a large, covered, rectangular arena with three large mirrors on the walls (which I hadn't noticed at all). One was at the short end near the sliding door at a corner, one centrally located on the far end wall and one halfway down the long side wall.

This was the final training experience and volunteers were called for. Of course, I was there to learn and just had to be doing, so I and two others stepped up, while the rest of the group observed.

The simple instruction was a 'mirror walk': to choose one or more horses, and to follow and mirror what the horse does, while reflecting on the qualities required for us to lead or facilitate this work, whatever that might mean to us.

The three of us stood motionless for a couple of minutes, mirroring the still horses who were without halters and free to move around as they wished. Then one horse began walking. *That's mine,* I thought. *It's moving, it's doing something, it's going somewhere.* I paired up with him and began to walk alongside at his shoulder.

The horse led me just a few paces to the corner end of the arena where we stopped. He looked outside through the narrow open doorway and smelt the air. I looked outside the narrow open doorway and smelt the air ... and we stood there, and stood there, and stood there.

My mind began thinking, *Ookaaay, we're standing here, come on, what next, what are we doing?*

So we stood there some more.

Then the horse pawed at the ground a few times, which generally means the horse is feeling some sort of impatience or tension and feels the need to move its feet, so I mirrored the horse, pawed at the ground, stamped my foot and asked the horse, "Why are you so impat—?" I hadn't even fully formed the word 'impatient' when I was struck by the realisation that it was not about the horse at all. It was me who was being impatient. Hmmm, okay; I let that thought go and we stood there in stillness, breathing together.

Lesson 1: Sometimes there's nowhere to go, nothing to do, except be here now, observe with all your senses, be fully present with your body, thoughts and breath.

Then the horse lifted its head, ears pricked forward, intently looking straight into the mirror slightly above and directly ahead of us. I hadn't noticed the mirror and so, mirroring the horse, I also looked into it.

It reflected the entire group, the rest of the herd, the other two participants standing alongside their horses, who hadn't moved, and the two trainers off near the far corner.

Okay, I thought, *what's important about this reflection?* I could see the whole group of horses and humans, some clumped in a group, others spread around.

Lesson 2: Pay attention to the whole environment. Practise shifting your attention between the big picture and the smaller details. Notice that some of the herd are together, others are off on their own. And you still don't have to control anything or do anything about this.

Upon this insight, the horse turned right and together we walked down the centre line, the entire length of the arena, directly to the mirror at the far end. Again the horse stopped, standing there with his ears pricked forward, looking intently into the second mirror. I did the same and could see the entire group but it was from a different point of view and this time I could also see the reflection of both the horse and myself.

Lesson 3: Remember to look at things from numerous points of view and take all opinions and viewpoints into account. What you think you're seeing changes when you observe from a different perspective and gather more information. As a leader, I am also part of the group; there is a two-way field effect and I am being impacted upon, while also impacting and reflected in, with and by others.

Then the horse turned back around, took a few steps, and turned left to take me to stand directly in front of the third mirror. It suddenly struck me that this was a 'mirror walk' and the horse had just led me directly to the third mirror! Coincidence? This time the reflection was just the horse and me. A deeply profound realisation hit me hard to the core, a gut punch that challenged my entire identity and beliefs. *Shit ... this is about me, isn't it? I've got lots more inner work to do.*

Lesson 4: In that moment I realised that I'd lived 47 years of my life being a total control freak. I had these false beliefs that everything I did had to be perfect, that I could never rely on anyone else and certainly never show weakness or appear vulnerable, that I had to always take charge and be in control in order to feel safe and worthy. It was also about tapping into both my inner and outer environment for gathering information.

Tears welled up in my eyes as, for the first time, I allowed and embraced that sense of vulnerability, of not knowing, of not being in control. I laid my hand on the horse's neck and spoke the words, "I give up control, you be the leader, I trust you. I will follow."

The horse turned around and we walked back to the centre of the arena. In all my years of contemplative practice, I'd never felt so complete, so whole, so present, so thoughtless yet full of sensory feeling as we did that walk. Only the horse and I existed; the rest of the group, the trainers, even the arena all disappeared from awareness.

Then the horse stopped and lowered his head, his nose running along from my knees down to and touching around and upon my feet to the ground. I felt a sense of being solidly grounded and an intense urge to kneel, to pay homage, to honour. To what, I didn't know exactly—to Horse? To nature? To presence? To life? To myself?

I knelt down and as I did the horse also knelt down beside me, wrapping his head around me in an embrace. It's hard to find the words that convey the power of my experience from this point. Here we were together, both kneeling in an embrace that exploded open my heart with an overwhelming, all-encompassing, full-body sensation of wholeness, love, compassion, acceptance, a sense that I am all that ever was or will be wrapped up together. It was so huge, so powerful that I was afraid I couldn't allow it, couldn't receive it, couldn't contain it, so there was a moment of resistance. How can I allow this much feeling in? I feared being totally overwhelmed and losing all sense of self and becoming a blubbering mess, only to realise that was exactly what I needed to do. This was about totally letting go of control of ... well, everything, my identity included, and simply receiving and allowing the feeling to express in and through me. With tears streaming down my face, this was ultimate vulnerability and with it deep and profound feelings of connectedness, and, dare I say it? Massive, total and completely overwhelming Oneness. I am whole. I am love.

After what seemed endless time, we both stood, and the horse led me directly back to the group, to my empty chair, picked the chair up in his mouth and then dropped it as if to say, "Okay, you're done" and wandered off to have a roll. I collapsed on the chair, gobsmacked and speechless, along with the 30 other people present. We didn't process or talk about what had just happened as the whole experience was just as much for everyone else as it was for me. Being present in the field of Horse, we were all part of, and contributed to, what had unfolded.

I don't know if it was a spiritual awakening or awakening to the spirit of Horse but my life changed. How much easier and less stressful it is to tap into the distributed intelligence of the body, to easily make decisions and to know what is driving that decision-making process. To live life not trying to organise and control everything, to trust others. To hold the idea that we are all already whole and not to deny others of their learning process by jumping in, fixing or rescuing them. To embrace not knowing, to connect with our compassionate heart desires and allow this to drive head-based creativity. That when you are not driven by survival energy and this inner communication, alignment and integration is in play, decision-making is easy, and inspired heart and gut-based courageous action naturally unfolds.

Truly generative and adaptive horsemanship, like leadership, or teaching or parenting or any profession that requires interactions with others, requires these whole new levels of self-awareness and self-facilitation for integrating head-based intellect with heart-based values and gut-based instincts. This is because the head, heart and gut brains represent and process very specific forms of intelligence and intuitive functions. All needing to be communicated with while in coherence and aligned and integrated for wise decisions and actions.

No longer can we, as re-evolving humans, rely solely on the competencies dominated by our head brains alone. Like a thriving herd, truly thriving and leading successfully in today's world requires 'whole heart-head-gut leaders' responding to, rather than reacting to, in the moment. You just need to allow a little space to check in and take that path from your heart to your head to your gut.

And that's okay. Life is a constant process of experiential learning. It's not a cycle, it's a spiral, with each experience, learning and reflection shaping us and contributing to our emerging wisdom.

I love how this process repeats. Our embryological development is also a spiral-like process, with each layer building on and interweaving with the other layers.

In closing, I'd love to share this Rumi quote as a touchstone to the Spirit of Horse.

'Out beyond ideas of wrongdoing and
Right doing, there is a field. I'll meet you there.
When the soul lies down in this grass ...'
Horse lives in this space, in the field.

My understanding is Rumi is saying that this is the space where we can reconnect with what has heart and meaning. Firstly with ourselves and then from there, with each other, other beings and the natural world. This is the space that opens up when we get curious, embracing the vulnerability that arises in not knowing and letting go of control, judgement and ideas we may have of how things should be, of good and bad, right and wrong.

Bodyfulness, and nervous system regulation in relationship, not just mindfulness.

It's taken me many years to really truly and deeply get this and, like everyone, I still do occasionally leave my body. Horse always reminds me of the importance of Being in the Field, and they do this with gentleness and joy and without bias or judgement. That's why I love sharing and facilitating this life leadership work through coaching and retreats. The insights we gain about how we show up are always unexpected and powerfully profound, and compassionate Horse is always there, fully present, waiting for us to return back home to ourselves.

If you'd like to evolve your ways of being, doing, feeling and thinking, for less stress and more joy and wisdom, come join us sometime and lie down on the grass. You will find us out standing in our field.

Become more Horse like, find your heart field and BE outstanding in it.

ABOUT THE AUTHOR
Cheryl Cruttenden

Cheryl Cruttenden is the founder of Windhorse Wisdom – Coaching and Embodied Leadership with Horses programs.

Possessing a lifetime of horse experience and background in outdoor education, Cheryl's head-based craving for science-informed practice is artfully weaved with psychoeducation, experiential learning, contemplative, and trauma-informed embodiment practices.

Sharing her work both locally and internationally, her style has been described as warm, safe, generous, engaging, transformative and even magical.

She is passionate about the power of nature-based learning in partnership with horses. Her facilitating skills, executive coach training and studies in somatic leadership practices help guide others to bring cognitive concepts and knowing from the head back down into the body.

Her work unfolds naturally and gently between horse, human and nature, harnessing potential and unbridling the human spirit in relationship and deep connection to the distributed intelligence of the body.

She also trains other coaches and leaders through both in-house and in-the-field certified mBIT coaching and training.

CONNECT WITH CHERYL

Website: *www.mbrainingwithhorses.com*
LinkedIn: *www.linkedin.com/in/cheryl-cruttenden-07428214*
Instagram: *www.instagram.com/cherylcruttenden*
Cheryl Cruttenden Facebook: *www.facebook.com/cheryl*
Windhorse Wisdom: *www.facebook.com/WindhorseWisdom*

MARTIN KRIPPNER

The Case For Volunteer Leadership: Getting The Best From Others When They're Not Obliged To Try

How dull it is to pause, to make an end, To rust unburnish'd, not to shine in use!
Ulysses by Alfred Lord Tennyson

I am pretty confident in suggesting that most of us scanning the pages of Wholehearted Leadership Revolution are looking for answers to questions that have vexed all sorts of leaders for thousands of years:

What does great leadership actually look like? What do I need to do? What works? What doesn't? What must I avoid? What must I embrace? How do I know when I'm leading well? When should I be 'nice' and when must I be firm? Am I up to the task or am I just another imposter hiding behind position and hierarchy? Will somebody please tell me?

In all honesty, I can only say I'm not sure what the answers are but, like any decent, well-meaning leader, I'm going to try to help you find them. When the facilitators of *Wholehearted Leadership Revolution* approached me about contributing this chapter my response was, "My God! Why are you asking me?

I don't know anything about leadership. I've just picked things up along the way." The Imposter Syndrome Early Warning System flicked to Code Red in record time.

So, what I set out to do here is outline my personal experiences to provide a fresh perspective on leadership, that may partially help with those big questions around the 'what' and the 'how' of leading others.

In 1998, with only two days' notice, I became head of the drama department in a large school. I had not taught much drama for a number of years, and I hardly knew the other teachers. I was daunted and flattered to be asked, rather reluctant but keen to give it a go. I had no idea what I was doing and was given no leadership advice, support or training. It was sink or swim. I sank. And I should be clear: this is no triumph over adversity, no noble try and try again, no 'journey' from failure to stellar success. It's about what I gradually learned while stumbling about in the dark, trying to find the light.

To some extent, this chapter will try to inform and help that 'me' who arrived at the drama department door in October 1998. I am going to set out what I wish someone had told me – the big handwaving stuff, the daily bits and pieces that add up to something truly substantial; the spectacular disasters that we later rationalise as 'opportunities for growth'. And from the outset, I will try to be honest – not easy when you write about yourself ...

Here goes.

After four months in the role, and once I felt vaguely on top of day-to-day activities, I decided to stage a large musical – something that had happened only once in the school's twenty years and, which was ten years before I arrived. The idea was to make a splash, enthuse the students and create a culture of inclusion, camaraderie and accessibility. I also wanted to please parents, impress my senior leaders and, most of all, give my many talented learners an opportunity to perform. On occasions, the world of the theatre can seem a little like a cult, where only the initiated and skilled can gain admittance. I wanted to change all that. I wanted to mount successful, stylish productions that would enthuse my students, encourage and foster a closer, collaborative culture across the whole school and create events that would promote it as a centre of creative excellence. Right from the start, it was about the process as much as the final product; this had to be fun, exciting, challenging and exacting all at once. I wanted the school community to enjoy the show and feel a shared sense of pride and achievement.

As a theatre director – particularly in a large-scale musical – your influence and expertise are both limited and defined. Your awareness must be broad but your focus narrow. High levels of trust and autonomy are needed because you must rely on the talent, judgement, knowledge and efforts of others. Mounting theatre is the ultimate team sport. It requires actors, wardrobe, front of house, choreographers, backstage crew, musicians, publicists, box office, make-up artists and technical experts to work collaboratively and comfortably. As in so many areas of work, the various roles needed for a large musical production attract a profoundly diverse group of workers. Rarely are musicians like front-of-house organisers, while make-up and wardrobe may have responsibility for how people look yet are usually very different types of human beings from each other. It goes without saying that even those doing the same job can be very different in their attitude, interests or levels of skill. Violinists and drummers are not the same, stage crew often have a quiet contempt for actors, and woe betide any director who gets on the wrong side of the backstage crew. Some actors are passionate, committed and driven; others are just there to have fun.

Along the way I made mistakes, bit off more than I could chew and experienced varying moments of self-doubt. Looking back, I saw how I focused way too much on outcomes rather than the needs and feelings of those around me. But somehow and gradually, over a period of years without much in the way of reflection or analysis, I began to apply leadership principles that worked for me more often than not. It was only many years later that I realised that those principles–created by failures, successes and moments in between – are applicable across all workplaces and hold true for human beings regardless of situation, circumstance, age, experience, role or skills.

Decades on from that first musical performance, a vivid string of memories burn bright: finishing the preparations and rehearsals only 50 minutes before curtain up on opening night; managing the moods of the biggest diva in the show (the orchestra drummer); the blossoming of anxious actors once they were certain they could rise to the occasion; the mixture of relief and sadness after the last show.

The department began to grow and gradually became a place of energy, ideas, excitement and accomplishment. The range of things we did expanded enormously, resulting in a much broader range of people involving themselves in dramatic activities. By focusing on processes rather than results, producing theatre became a happier, less strident pursuit encouraging and supporting rather than demanding excellence.

Because of the unique nature of theatre, the conscious things I incorporated gradually evolved into a clear set of principles and practices. It was only many years later, when I moved into adult Learning and Development, that I realised that what I had done to make things work were not unique to amateur theatre at all – they were universal truths that could be applied to any human endeavour which required a group of people to come together to reach a goal, fulfil a requirement or achieve an outcome. I used the techniques for amateur dramatic performance, but it took years of subsequent experiences and work challenges before I realised applying volunteer principles to any work situation – whether voluntary or professional – could achieve:

- success and high-performing outcomes,
- emotionally satisfying experiences for team members,
- sustainable ways of working,
- a culture of thriving that encourages discretionary effort,
- a model for leading in a way that is positive, affirming and rewarding for leaders.

Let's now explore the parameters of the concept of Volunteer Leadership. What does this actually mean?

1. If people are volunteering, they are not formally obliged to recognise a hierarchy and follow directions. They do not receive remuneration or professional recognition for their efforts – doing the work does not pay the mortgage or put bread on the table. Indeed, often voluntary work can COST the worker through time, money and labour. They choose to do the work and can just as easily choose not to do it. Most importantly, they can leave at any time.
2. Leading volunteers successfully requires a deep conscious awareness that the experience MUST provide an array of intrinsic rewards and a shared and individual sense of satisfaction and achievement. Of course, this is true of most human endeavours but is more acute

when no material rewards will flow from the volunteer's labour, effort or achievement.
3. A simple truth: if people, as volunteers, are not obliged to stay, they are less compelled and governed by rules, procedures or requirements. This may sound strange, even extreme, but it is exactly what I had to cope with mounting a range of productions several times a year for nearly ten years.

So what are the lessons that we can take from voluntary work and apply to a professional, renumerated context? And here's the essential point: the things that make a good (or bad, for that matter) voluntary working experience are the things that create good (or bad) professional working experiences.

Now comes the challenge of successfully applying volunteer leadership concepts to a formal, professional work context. Undoubtedly, two complementary things must occur:

1. The rewards of paid professional labour MUST be replaced by something else.
2. The expectations and assumptions of hierarchy need to be reshaped to fit a different form of work contract.

Earlier, I suggested very few of us read books on leadership to feel enriched or entertained. We pick them up because we want answers: skills, insights and/ or techniques. We want to build a philosophy of leadership and hone a series of skills and behaviours that achieve operational success, develop others and give us a sense of satisfaction.

So, at this stage four questions worth asking ourselves are:

- **Question 1:** Could you, or would you, manage and lead in the way you currently do if team members could walk away at any moment?
- **Question 2:** Do you find yourself thinking (or even saying) something along the lines of "I am the boss, and you will do as I say"?

- **Question 3:** Can you, and do you, articulate where we are going and why we are going there, what Paul Keating famously called "the vision thing"?
- **Question 4:** In what sense is every member of our team equal – regardless of skill, responsibility, age or experience?

These rather confrontational questions are essential to embracing and applying volunteer leadership behaviours. The answers require humility, grace, honesty and courage. By asking ourselves these questions, we embrace the concept of leader as servant and manager as supporter.

All around us, it is evident that with the evolution of the Digital Age, the rate of change is accelerating and the need for adaptability has never been greater. I would contest that Industrial Age ways of working, where we defined ourselves by what we did, how well we did it and our place in the hierarchy, are being rapidly eroded. But with the loss of so many old certainties, we have a golden opportunity to reimagine work. And why not imagine work as something we want to do, because at work we can embrace the human hunger to be genuinely creative, and proudly and confidently autonomous? It is in our working lives where we can add value, make a difference and ward off those vile demons of human existence: loneliness and lack of purpose.

It is clear that changes to old ways of working have been hugely accelerated by the massive disruption COVID has brought to so many sectors of society. Organisations in the post-COVID era ignore the emotions and needs of their people at their peril. Almost overnight, a profoundly new industrial landscape has emerged where people are used to – and increasingly demand – flexibility, autonomy, a positive work-life balance, and leaders who collaborate and encourage rather than command and control. Just as remote working has become more broadly accepted, it is also increasingly demanded by employees.

Knowledge workers now have access to jobs all around the world and there is every indication that this trend will continue and grow. Digital Age workers have choices and clearly feel empowered to walk at any moment if they receive a better offer – just like volunteers. Gone (or going) are the days when a handful of leaders make all the decisions, and the rest of the organisation is required to fall into step behind. The traditional extrinsic rewards and punishment motivations are no longer enough – knowledge workers are demanding a greater sense of purpose, more autonomy and collaborative work structures. In addition, the modern world of work is very complex, with far too many areas of expertise required to reach success and meet the expectations of consumers, stakeholders and other end clients. Modern leaders need their workers to contribute more rather than just be blind followers. They need their employees to *want* to be there, to 'volunteer' not just their time but their expertise, otherwise they will at best contribute only the bare minimum and, at worst, find greener pastures elsewhere.

This is where volunteer leadership principles come in, and by embracing them leaders can create the right culture and emotional context for individuals to thrive, feel valued, creatively solve problems and be comfortable with change.

The Why of Volunteer Leadership

Life is a worry and it's constant – the worry, I mean. Life? Not so much – and, of course, that's a huge worry too. Sometimes worrying is helpful, even valuable, but usually it isn't. Occasionally we need to worry – to identify risks, avoid disasters and appropriately apportion effort and industry. Yet so much of our worry is unproductive, futile and, all too often, unnecessary.

It seems to me we humans generally worry about four things:

1. Survival, mortality and ageing
2. Our status and place in the pecking order
3. Work
4. Love and relationships

Of course, we may also concern ourselves with getting the washing done or why our children are so reluctant to take our advice, but these four are the biggies.

I am not equipped or qualified to offer anything much on the first – except to say eat your fruit and vegetables, pray if you think that helps, and find some exercise you can enjoy and stick at. As for the second, recognise that while lots of (undeserving) others may be wealthier, more attractive, more successful or more talented than us – that's just the way it is and, no, it's not fair – there will always be many who are much less so. Any way you look at it, trying to alleviate status anxiety is a bit of a fool's errand because 'every time you think you might be winning the rat race, they invent faster rats.'

So let's focus on the last two: work and love and relationships.

It's stating the obvious to say that two of the most important human preoccupations governing our thinking and emotions are love and work. We worry a great deal about both, we expend so much energy on both and we endlessly fantasise about success in both. In large measure, it is love and work that brings us joy and self-regard or despair and self-loathing. Not exclusively but in large measure, love and work give our lives meaning, definition and comfort. And the application of Volunteer Leadership principles can effectively channel those profound human needs to provide the surest, easiest and most sustainable method for achieving success for organisations, individuals and us as leaders.

Reducing worry about love, relationships and work is a pretty daunting task, but I have a quiet optimism that some of the things leaders can do may help a little. If we aspire to become Wholehearted Leaders – and if you are reading this book, that probably means you are – we must have the courage and the belief to tackle major issues, demonstrate our humanity, and recognise that life in all its rich complexity is perennially challenging for all of us all of the time.

And here's the lovely irony: the less we worry about work and relationships, the more we can mitigate our anxieties surrounding mortality and status.

After 25 years, I decided I had done about as much as I could in teaching and I took up a learning and development role as a trainer and facilitator in the public sector. Over a number of years, I have presented a workshop called *Building High Performance* 87 times to large and small teams across the Australian public service sector and a combined audience of around 1600 people. Early in the workshop, participants are asked to reflect on their best-ever working experience. Very quickly, a remarkable pattern emerges – people will list the same four things:

1. My work had purpose and meaning – I made a difference and I added value.
2. High, comforting levels of trust and collaboration existed within my team and I felt welcomed, appreciated and connected to others.
3. I was working hard, I was challenged and engaged, I had autonomy and I cared or to use a modern phrase – I was emotionally invested.
4. Although the work was hard, we laughed a lot and had fun.

To reiterate, these responses were not just common or frequent, they were invariable. More than 1600 people – regardless of age, gender, hierarchy, education, personal experience or cultural background – referenced the same things. Remarkably, on a regular basis, both men and women are moved and quickly become emotional telling their stories. Some can clearly recall the people and the bonds within the team but remember little about the actual work. Others go into great detail, describing the intricacies of what they did, the camaraderie, the sense of achievement and the joy of connection. And every story incorporates a hugely emotional dimension – it seems it just cannot be our best work time if we leave our emotions at the front door. It bears mention that when people reminisce, they almost always assume it was the accident of having a great bunch of 'nice' people brought together by luck and circumstance that was such a significant reason for this miraculous best-ever working experience. Rarely do we conclude that a welcoming culture, benign and generous leadership, defined team purpose and inclusive behaviours might be creating the 'niceness'.

Almost as noteworthy, is what was NOT expressed during those 87 workshops. Not one person ever has said, "We did very little except play computer games, ate hot chips and watched TV." Nor have I heard, "I turned up, did my job and then went home."

A further aside worth noting – when I began presenting *Building High Performance* I would also ask participants to describe their worst-ever working experience. However, so many people would become quite distressed very quickly – and remain so – that I decided to abandon the exercise. This reinforces the observation made earlier: work involves an emotional element for human beings regardless of how much we try to appear detached, cool under pressure or professional. We must not deny this emotional element but harness it to unleash human creativity, operational success, kindness, connection and self-worth.

While working on unsalaried projects requires different approaches and overcoming a number of obstacles, it also has a range of innate benefits. People are usually keenly motivated, outcome-focused, and happy to contribute and collaborate. Long-term grievances are rare, and people choose to be a part of the endeavour. Above all, they care. The project matters to cast, crew and support staff. In the theatre, the project is finite, tangible and clearly defined, and the goals are generally shared: we want to put on a great show, achieve audience acclaim and enjoy both the rehearsal process and the performance.

This is all to illustrate the way in which volunteer work complements employees' *intrinsic* motivations and thus lends itself well to eliciting the four outcomes that participants in my workshops reported as representing their best-ever working experiences. And by thinking of your paid team members as 'volunteers', you can tap into those same innate benefits.

Volunteer Leadership Principles

This brings us to the principles of volunteer leadership that worked for me in encouraging the four outcomes above, and can work for you:

1. Articulate the mission, vision and goal, over and over.
2. Give employees a definite, clear purpose, a designated role, and key responsibilities.
3. Recognise the critical human need for belonging, camaraderie and connection.
4. Balance collaboration AND autonomy – i.e., the things that create trust.
5. Encourage, recognise and show appreciation, frequently.
6. Actively choose to have fun and laugh.
7. Ask questions and appreciate the answers.

8. Demonstrate empathy and take time to listen – to feelings, struggles, doubts and ideas.
9. Understand the need people have for certainty, planning and responsibility.
10. Provide clear job instructions if needed (but get out of the way if not).
11. Be adaptable, flexible, and comfortable with ambiguity.
12. Show forgiveness when others stumble and apologise when you do.

The 'How' of Volunteer Leadership

Now we have come to the tricky part. It is one thing to know what actions to take and essential to know why they matter, but putting them into practice? Ah, there's the rub!

The process is hardly simple at first glance– because we are dealing with that most complex of phenomena: human beings – but I would humbly suggest that it can be relatively straightforward.

Step one: It's not about you, it's about them. As leaders, we must focus on the human needs of team members – those things all of us need when we are working.

- Outcome 1: Where *I shine in use:* purpose, meaning, where I add value and make a difference: my contribution – the bit that's mine.
- Outcome 2: An inclusive culture of trust, camaraderie, collaboration and connection = my team, my people – what Tennyson referred to as *"One equal temper of heroic hearts... [who share a goal] ...strong in will, to strive to seek, to find, and not to yield."*
- Outcome 3: A sense of engagement, passion and effort: I wasn't just doing a job – I cared because it mattered.
- Outcome 4: The work was not always easy, but I laughed a lot and had fun. Underrated and undervalued by far too many human beings, it is fun and laughter that are the escape valves for tension, anxiety and fear and it is utterly essential. Always remember: *if you can laugh together, you can work together.*

These are the things that people need to achieve real, sustainable success—always have, always will.

Step Two: This is where we shift our attention to us – our behaviours, the outcomes we wish to see, what we need to encourage and discourage within our teams – the Twelve Principles of Volunteer Leadership. We must ask ourselves; *Do I really listen to my people and demonstrate empathy? Do I encourage, articulate a vision, demonstrate forgiveness, apologise, value autonomy, show appreciation and celebrate the success of others? Do I do these things in a sustained, committed and ongoing manner?*

Step Three: In order to transplant the principles of Volunteer Leadership into the paid work context I would suggest that nothing less than a sophisticated mental sleight of hand is required. We need to adopt the following 'what if' premise by imagining that:

1. Your people could walk at any time and you are powerless to stop them. It is their thoughts, feelings and experience that determine whether they keep turning up and getting stuff done or decide to jump ship. And while you may not be responsible for everything your people experience, you most certainly become responsible if they walk.
2. You cannot rely on a hierarchy and clear structure to get things done. How might your values shift? What might you need to be mindful of?
3. Your leadership is solely reliant on your diplomacy and powers of persuasion. How's your ego? Are you able to balance the needs of others with your own attitudes to leadership and view of yourself?

Step Four: I mentioned earlier that adopting and applying these insights did not magically happen overnight for me as a leader of volunteers. The concepts gradually seeped into my actions through trial, error, mistakes and success. Ironically, the most transformational application of Volunteer Leadership is not about what we do as leaders, it is about our capacity to step back, let go and trust in others. Ultimately, it becomes not what we do but what we *don't do*.

Perhaps a further example may help explain the concept. In October 2001, we were up against it. We had staged a brave, exciting Australian musical in May to recognise the centenary of Federation. The show had been a great success, so much so we were asked in October to be part of the entertainment for a Women in Politics national conference. We only had a short period of time to rehearse, and I had to accept that near enough was good enough. It was touch and go at times. I just couldn't do it all myself. I had to delegate and trust that others had the commitment, skills and confidence to do their bit. This was the true test of the principles in place. I had no choice but to step back and let go. My role became that of cheerleader, to boost the confidence of others and help them believe that we could pull it off in such a short period of time. I am writing this 22 years later, but I remember the night like it was yesterday. My cast and crew rose to the challenge, brought the house down, and received a standing ovation from 620 women – including the Attorney General, various ministers and a number of other federal politicians. What resonates so strongly more than twenty years on is not so much what I did, but the value of delegating, trusting and then *getting out of the way.*

Volunteer Leadership principles provide a clear picture of what leaders need to address in an ever more dynamic world of work. The pace of change has been remarkable in a very short time and there is every indication that the take-up of flexible, adaptable work practices will be sustained and even accelerated in the future. And while almost everything is changing at breakneck speed, we must never forget that one thing does not – human nature. Human fears, the needs of people and the things that make us comfortable and comforted, purposeful and engaged, those things remain constant. Leaders ignore human nature at their peril. We know what human beings– individually and collectively – require and desire to feel engaged and satisfied. As leaders, it is our task, our privilege and our burden to help provide it for them.

And let us never forget: **There is no limit to what we can do or where we can go if we don't mind who gets the credit.**

ABOUT THE AUTHOR
Martin Krippner

Martin Krippner is a much sought-after trainer, negotiator, facilitator and leader of leaders, whose reputation proceeds him in the Australian public sector.

Martin has trained many thousands of leaders around Australia in negotiation, conflict resolution, presentation, leadership skills and high-performance team creation, among other areas of expertise. He uses his impressive background in leading complex theatrical productions to inform his craft. Martin is often asked to facilitate high-profile events that require his mastery of group dynamics and servant leadership.

It is also worth noting that even at the most serious and portentous events, Martin believes passionately in the power of fun and laughter to bring human beings together.

Martin lives with his three daughters in Canberra, in the Australian Capital Territory. When he's not facilitating, he enjoys classical music, the theatre or cruising the countryside in his beloved convertible, wind blowing through his ... *scarf.*

CONNECT WITH MARTIN

Email: *kripym@gmail.com*

ANDREW LIZZIO
Shining Brightly

It was the morning after. My heart sank in my chest as I wondered if it had all been a bad dream. I sat there frozen, daring not to open my eyes. Eventually, I did, and the harsh reality of yesterday flooded back.

Viv lay there, motionless, heavily sedated. Forcing myself out of the plastic hospital chair, I stood up and slowly stretched the kinks out of my back. *This is fucked up,* I thought as I watched him sleep. The young doctor doing the rounds that night saw that I was awake, and he dropped his head in the hope of avoiding eye contact. "Doctor," I pleaded, "anything, please!"

"Well, I have to be honest; things are not looking good. We need to do more tests, but it appears that his L2 and L3 vertebrae are shattered, and his spinal cord has been completely severed. I doubt if he will ever walk again." The words delivered by the doctor were like a sledgehammer to my chest. Seeing the distress on my face, he added, "… but you never know. There are advances in medicine every day, and he appears to be in good health." He scribbled a few quick notes on Viv's charts, returned the clipboard to the bed-end, and escaped at a half sprint.

It took days for the reality to sink in. *My best friend, now a paraplegic,* I thought as the darkness started to engulf me. No more fishing. No more hiking. The memories of us walking the Kokoda trail last year turned to shades of grey as my mind attempted to void the beauty of that experience.

For months I stayed by his bedside, adding what little comfort I could. That's when my inner voice became an inner scream. *What are you doing?! Are you going to accept him for who he now is?* The way the question was framed in my head was not really a question at all but a call to action. Swamped in feelings of loneliness, boredom and helplessness, I saw a glimmer of hope. *No, I'm NOT going to accept him! I'm going to FIX him.* Not one of my proudest moments, deciding to choose the lesser path because it made me feel of value.

So off I set on my egotistical journey, devouring any information I could get my hands on, from exoskeletons to the latest in stem cell research. I came up empty, and that feeling of value was engulfed by this looming darkness yet again. I could not believe that with all the technical advances of the human race, there was almost nothing done for people with mobility problems. Even the wheelchair was still basically the same since it was invented almost 400 years ago.

My heart sank further into the darkness as I realised that the world generally did not care for the disadvantaged. *This is not right!* And at that moment, I asked myself probably the hardest, most important self-defining question of my life, *are you going to do the right thing?* To me, this was not a fork in the road; it was more like a train smashing into me, sending me flying over a cliff to eventually land on a rocky goat trail full of pain and suffering. It scared the crap out of me. But I had to see this through, not just for Viv but for myself. Owning that commitment, I picked myself back up, brushed off the dirt of a thousand reasons why I shouldn't, and focussed on the reason why I should:

It is the right thing to do!

And at that moment, I passed my first lesson in becoming a leader: committing to lead myself. From that point onwards, my mantra in life became, 'Do the right thing, at the right time, with the right people, no matter the pain.' Just then, I had no idea how important this decision would be for me in the future, saving my life in two near-suicide attempts. That goat trail got rough in places!

How could I get Viv walking again? The thought was constant in my head, not willing to let it go for anything. Not only were there no solutions for people with mobility problems but there was nothing in any other industry that could possibly help. So I did what I always do in these situations: let the solution come to me. As I closed my eyes, it started like it always did, like a child playing with a toy for the first time, getting feelings of excitement and confusion at the same time. I inhaled a deep breath, held it for a few seconds, then slowly relaxed and let all the stress exit with the escaping breath. And not just the stress, but letting go of all that I am, or more importantly, all that I think I am. Letting go of all the noise, all the voices in my head until there is nothing but stillness. No fear. No insecurities. A place of sacred beauty and limitless potential. The place where magic happens.

It felt as though no time at all had passed when I opened my eyes. *That's so obvious,* I thought as my thinking brain tried to play catch-up with the imagery of my mind's eye. But I needed help and lots of it. Soon enough, I found myself buried deep in human anatomy, studying the mechanics of skeletal muscles. And that's when the final piece of the puzzle fell into place to reveal for the first time how systems of behaviours emerge instead of being designed. How to look at the interactions of components instead of looking at the components themselves. That is, don't design the solution, design the components so that when a critical mass of them interacts, the desired solution emerges. So simple, why had this not been done before? Had it been done before? I had to know.

I started devouring countless research papers over the internet, reading through mountains of patents around the world, but I found nothing that even came close. Exhausted, I slumped back into my computer chair, put my head in my hands and thought, *this can't be happening!* My fingers started to shake as they automatically reached for the keyboard. *Could this actually work? How could it NOT work? This is the mechanics of nature itself.* So I closed my eyes, took a deep breath, and I got to work. I knew what I had to do. I was about to invent a new form of bionic technology, one that could not only get Viv walking again but running, dancing, jumping, and so much more.

It took about one week to create a computer simulation based on the interaction of muscle cells and another two weeks to write a research paper describing this new concept. Finishing late one night, it was tools down. Done! Now I just had to wait for the world to wake up so that I could show someone. I lay on the floor next to my computer with my eyes closed and my mind open, not sleeping a wink.

The next morning, I was on the phone organising catchups with some of my most trusted scientist and engineering friends. To my surprise, their feedback was split and polarised. "Andrew, I cannot see this working at all!" or "Andrew, you are a genius! This will change the world." And it was then that I knew I had something. This polarization of professional opinions is what I look for. For me, especially in situations where the solution is complex, it means that the people who don't understand the fundamentals think that the solution is ridiculous. But for the ones that do, it's massive.

I spent the next six months without a life. A typical day for me was: 3 am bounding out of bed, too excited about some idea I had during the night about bionics; 6 am, down tools and get ready for work; 7 am, start my regular job as a computer enterprise architect; 7 pm, arrive home, have dinner in front of the computer or pick at something on a plate while I was building the world's first bionic arm; 10 pm, unable to keep my eyes open, drift off to sleep, sometimes on the computer keyboard. My wife knew that this was what made me, me, and she gave 100% support whenever she could. I started attracting money and people to accelerate the development of this technology. I represented Australia for innovation over two consecutive years in the USA and China, respectively. I was approached by TEDx to tell my story, but Rob (my IP lawyer and good friend) got me to rip up the contract for fear that the patents were not secure enough around the world.

I had to wait for another three years until I got a call from Rob saying, "I hope you are sitting down! I have just witnessed something I've never seen before. You wrote this patent, right?" "Yes, of course. Where's this going, Rob?" He said, "Well, I've got the response back from the USA and Europe here in my hand, and I cannot believe it. Normally this process takes years, going back and forth between their lawyers and us to work out what part of this idea is original. And here's the kicker. It came back without dispute." "So what?" I said without understanding why he was so excited. "Andrew, getting a patent passed without dispute means that no one has ever come up with anything like this before. I have never seen a patent get accepted in this way. Not in all my years of practising patent law. It is incredibly rare to witness the creation of an original idea. You must be a genius!"

I eventually put the phone down with a shaking hand, not understanding what had actually happened. And the nickname 'genius', which I hated so much, had now become my call sign from that day onwards, whether I liked it or not.

The next few years were interesting, to say the least. But before that, there is a backstory that needs airing, and it goes to the heart of why I am definitely NOT a 'genius', just a person able to sit in stillness with a passion for being wholehearted.

Mum walked with me, holding my hand for the one-block journey from home to school. Neither of us said a word, just looked at our feet shuffling on the pavement, knowing that this was going to be our first day apart. When we arrived at the front gate, she bent down and gave me a kiss. "It'll be alright, you know!" she said as she looked into my eyes. The tears welling up in her eyes dissolved any hope of me holding mine back, and they gushed out. She gave me a hug, turned around and walked off, trying to hide her own tears. As she turned the corner, I felt alone for the first time in my life.

As I stood by the gate in a daze, the school bell rang. Looking in the direction of that unpleasant noise, I saw a nun holding the large wooden handle of a heavy brass bell with both hands, shaking it commandingly. "Line up, children. Everyone in order! I want to see everyone on their best behaviour." Walking through the gate, I hurried along to join the line of 13 children about to enter my Year 1 classroom.

"You can sit there," the nun said, directing me to a seat in the second row. "That's your seat for the rest of the year." Looking up at her, I noticed that she was the same nun that rang the school bell. She stood erect, like one of those people who were taught correct walking posture by balancing a book on their head. "Okay, everyone, get out your writing books," she commanded, just like how she rang the school bell. "My name is Sister Bridget, and we are going to learn how to write the letter 'a'," she insisted. Slowly, she scratched out the letter on the front blackboard as the chalk complained with several odd and unpleasant squeaks. Putting down the chalk, she picked up a slender piece of bamboo cane and slapped it hard where the letter 'a' was sitting alone on the blackboard. "Turn to the first page and write the letter 'a'." I reached into my bag all excited and pulled out my fully complete writing book, placed it on the table and turned to the first page. My mum was a teacher, so the week before school started, she taught me how to write.

Sister Bridget slowly walked up the aisle, looking from side to side, tapping her bamboo cane on the floor to match her footsteps. Tap, tap, tap; I heard until she got to mine. The tapping stopped. She bent down and picked up my book, flicked through the pages and put it back down on the desk. Looking up at her, anticipating praise, she whacked her cane across my hands quicker than I could see. The sound was deafening. I will never forget as it swooshed through the air ending with a loud crack on my hand. "How DARE you finish your year's work, wasting a perfectly good workbook. I'll be telling your parents about this. Just you wait and see." She walked to her desk at the front of the room, got out a new workbook and headed back to me.

Confusion filled my head as silent tears welled up. My hands were shaking and throbbing where the cane had hit. "Here's another," she spat as she dropped the new workbook in front of me. "And this time, fill it out in class." I fumbled for my pencil, eventually picking it up just like Mum taught me, turned to the first page and started to write. Whack! Pain screamed through my left hand, and this time I wailed out in pain, not able to keep it in. "And that's for writing with the Devil's Hand. Rub it out, change hands and start again."

My right hand fumbled for the pencil, eventually picking it up. I struggled to see the page through my tears. Scratching out the letter 'a', I heard that whooshing sound once again, and I flinched as it connected with my shoulder. "That is the worst letter 'a' I have ever seen. Rub it out and do it again."

The rest of the day, I sat in silence, confused, not knowing the right thing to do. That day felt like it was never going to end as I watched each second tick over on the large black-and-white clock hanging at the front of the classroom. I breathed a sigh of relief as the final bell rang, carefully packed my bag, strapped it over my shoulders and escaped. Mum was waiting at the gate where she left me that morning. I could tell she'd been waiting for some time, dying to hear every detail of my day. I walked up to her, held her hand and motioned her to start walking. I said nothing and kept my head down low so that she could not see my cried-out eyes. That night at the dinner table, I told my story.

Dad got up from his chair, walked to the kitchen drawer and pulled out the wooden spoon. Whack! "If the nuns thought you deserved the cane, then here's another. They are the hand of God, and what they say is therefore true."

From that day onward, I kept it all bottled up inside. No friends and not daring to speak to anyone, I quickly became a recluse.

Halfway through Year 2, we got a replacement nun. "Okay, everyone. Silence!" Sister Bridget commanded. "You have a new teacher for two weeks while I am away. Make sure that you are on your best behaviour because I'll know if you aren't." The new nun's name was Sister Nardia, and she was young and beautiful, like an angel. As Sister Bridget left, Sister Nardia started doing the rounds by looking at our progress. When she got to mine, she gently moved my timid hand, hiding the answer. " Well done. You must be smart!" she said with sincerity. For the first time since my mum taught me how to write, someone actually showed interest. With this new burst of energy, the next two weeks were joyous, and my grades went from class dummy to class leader. As other children saw how quickly I was learning, they turned to me for help. I loved it and wanted more. This was my first taste of leadership.

But just as it started, it finished with Sister Bridget's return. My grades and motivation quickly returned to 'normal'. Home was not a pleasant environment either, with my father coining the phrase, "Yet again, Andrew, you are a disappointment," repeated for many years thereafter.

This was my first life lesson in being a Wholehearted Leader, understanding the value of nurtured inspiration.

The following four years of primary school followed a similar pattern: cane every day, commanded every hour, silenced every minute. That is until my second last year of primary school. Everything was about to change, and not for the better. For the next two years, I would be sexually molested at school on a regular basis. A fact that I kept hidden for 40 years. Every day I longed to leave that place, to finally escape the pain and confusion. That day finally came when I started Year 8 at the local public high school, hoping for even a small improvement. Sadly, there was none. Being the skinny, quiet kid, one type of pain was simply substituted for another as I was quickly targeted by the bullies. Fortunately, I was able to find solitude in the school library every lunch period, the only place the bullies dared not go.

I was shipped off to boarding school in Years 11 and 12. The bullying kicked up a notch. I was locked in cupboards, urinated on and, many broken bones later, including from my sister, I was still alone with no friends and no family support. I graduated from school with barely enough scholastic grades to study Computer Science at university. My first year was tough, not knowing who I was or what I wanted to do with my life. But for the first time in my life, I was not living in fear. End-of-year exams came and went, and it was now holiday time back with my family. A few weeks later, my dad handed me a letter from the university. It was my exam results. I opened it with trepidation, knowing that this was not going to be pretty. My father's words echoed in my head, freezing my thoughts. He glanced down at the piece of paper, and without a word, he walked away. Anything would have been better than that deafening silence and the sound of his boots on the wooden floor echoing abandonment.

Looking back at my exam results, I noticed something odd. The first-year mathematics exam had a 'conditional pass' stamped next to it, which meant I had another chance. With nothing else to do during the Christmas break, I picked up the thousand-page maths book, sat under a tree and turned to the first page. It was a slow start, taking about a week to read the first 20 pages, but then something clicked. I started to see patterns, and suddenly everything became simple and intuitive. Thoughts of Sister Nardia flooded my head. This time I gave myself permission to succeed. Before I knew it, I had devoured that book. Needless to say, I smashed the exam. University, from that point, got easier, as little by little, I allowed myself to shine.

The next year at university, I had enough knowledge and confidence to tutor Year 11 and 12 maths students. The first student arrived at my doorstep, ready to escape the pain of being labelled 'class dumbo'. I felt his pain and froze, remembering the horrors of Sister Bridget. At that same moment, I felt Sister Nardia's warm hand on my shoulder, inspiring me. With that feeling, I knew I could help him. I listened for anything that might inspire him, and as I did, his pain started to lift, attention increased, and passion became evident. It was not long before he was top of the class, and that made my heart sing. I tried that same approach on the next student, and the next, and so on, all with the same result. It became clear to me that learning was less about the content and more about inspiration. That is, not 'what' they were learning but 'why' they were learning it.

This was my second life lesson in being a Wholehearted Leader – understanding and respecting each person's uniqueness, what drives them, and their passions.

Just as quickly as university started, it finished. I started working as a computer programmer for a small company maintaining pharmacy and doctors' computer systems. The work was hard, with long hours, but I loved it. The feeling of responsibility was intoxicating. It was all about the outcome, not the output or how long it took.

As the company grew, middle management was needed to help with the burden of administration. Everyone suddenly had to do timesheets, were assigned tasks and performance managed instead of just doing what needed to be done. Responsibility seemed to be turned off like a light switch, ruthlessly converted to accountability. Company culture quickly changed from leading the staff to managing the staff as behaviour changed from 'want to' to 'have to'. I often heard others say, "Do you remember when we could walk into the boss's office and discuss what needs to be done? Now we have to justify everything to some pen-pusher who has no idea about anything! Don't they trust us anymore? This place is going to shit!" Within three months, there was a mass exodus. I ended up leaving too.

Another valuable wholehearted lesson for me – inspire people to 'want to' rather than 'have to'.

I quickly mastered my skills of pattern thinking, able to solve problems that no one else could, but that came with its limitations. I was not built for remembering names or numbers, learning another language, or not getting lost when there was more than one street. If I could not find a pattern in something, then, within seconds, it was gone as if it never existed. That, coupled with my lack of social skills, should have made me completely unemployable, but the opposite happened. Organisations everywhere wanted my services. They all needed to solve their unique set of problems, increase profit, or dominate a market or competitor. At last, I had found my value, my purpose in life. I was finally wanted. To be honest, I did not really care. I was of value. My father's voice in my head quietened ever so slightly.

But that feeling of value was short-lived. In fact, it made things worse. The problems I was solving were often at the executive level, which meant that I needed to communicate and, more importantly, demonstrate purpose and inspiration. As I was already somewhat familiar with purpose and inspiration, it didn't take me long to hone those skills. After all, purpose and inspiration were all about listening, and I had been doing that all my life. Communication and leadership, on the other hand, were a whole different kettle of fish.

Teams of people from various organisations across Australia were assigned to me, expecting me to lead them. Without knowing any better, I did the only thing I knew – lead by command. As you may have guessed, things did not start smoothly, but at that moment, I had a revelation: Thank you, Sister Bridget, for showing me the way. Weaving together how she made me feel with the mass exodus experienced in my first job, I came up with a solution. But it was going to come at a cost.

The next day I gathered the teams in the boardroom, took a deep breath and held it for a bit, then slowly let it out. It seemed to help calm my nerves slightly. "I have a problem," I said quietly under my breath. Looking up, I realised that no one heard me, so I shouted, "I have a problem!" The room went suddenly quiet. All eyes focused on me. "I am not good with names. In fact, I'm what they call a 'basket case' when it comes to names. And …" I went on, exposing my vulnerabilities. After I finished, there was an awkward silence in the room. I had to think fast, so I said, "Now it's your turn to talk about your vulnerabilities. Or just talk about anything that may be bothering you. But when you do, try only making statements about yourself, and try only asking questions of the other person."

They reluctantly turned to one another, more so as a joke and started their conversations. Within a very short period of time, the mood of the room changed entirely. For the first time, they were truly engaging with each other. We came to know each other in a way we had never known before, more than just recognising each other's professional skills. We saw each other's vulnerabilities and passions and, in doing so, created trust bonds that have not been broken to this day. It was at that point that we came together as a team, and I stepped up from being a commander to a trusted leader. Soon enough, I was being flown around the country for work, as well as giving talks to audiences of thousands around the world. I would never have imagined that such a single act of bravery would have led to such a life-defining pivot.

And there lies my next lesson in Wholehearted Leadership – never underestimate the power of vulnerability to instil trust. Trust is the essence of leadership.

It all seemed to be coming together nicely for me. People wanted to be part of my team, and organisations wanted my unique ability to fix them. However, life had other plans for me.

That's when everything changed due to a slippery tree branch. Viv fell six meters to the ground, landing on his shoulder, snapping his back in half with his legs dangling loosely over his head. He was rushed to hospital, and when I made it to his bedside, he said with a smile, "I suppose people weren't meant to fly" That moment marked a turning point in my career as I reassessed what's really important in life. Instead of 'what' I should be doing, it was replaced with 'why' I should be doing it. Sitting by Viv's bedside for months gave me the time that I needed to consider that question. Admittedly, I started off on the wrong foot, trying to fix him. But life has a funny way of giving you your next step, and it took me in a direction I would have never imagined.

Because I was developing it in my spare time, years passed as I developed this unique and exciting bionic technology. I did ask myself, *is working on it in my spare time the right thing to do? Why am I spending most of my time in a job that has little to do with my passions or my ethics, only to work on what I really want when I'm exhausted?* That's when the full impact of 'doing the right thing' really set in. It's NOT about convenience; it's about doing the right thing at the right time. The answer was clear, but so was the pain hiding behind it. I had a failing marriage, a huge house mortgage, and very little savings. There were a thousand good reasons for 'why not?' but only one compelling reason for 'why?'

My wife and I agreed on a separation. I quit my job and left everything behind except for a small bag of clothes and a toothbrush. Shivers flowed down my spine, knowing that, as a grown man, I was about to move back in with my parents. As I boarded the plane, I received a phone call from them saying that the COVID pandemic had hit our small hometown and that I'd be placed in quarantine for two weeks. Fortunately for me, quarantine was the old family beach house in a quiet coastal town that had one shop and one street – not the worst place to be stuck for a bit.

I enjoyed the peace and tranquillity and the getting back to nature. It took me a while to get used to the solitude of my own company, and I suppose I never really did. Every day I'd spend long hours researching and advancing the bionic technology. I found that I was very productive in this environment, so I asked my parents' permission to stay at the beach house a little longer. They agreed, and I slowly started converting the house to suit my passion. Friends who visited said, "This is not a house; it's a science lab with a kitchen!" Every day I'd experience colossal failures and massive successes, a real emotional rollercoaster. And every day, I'd pick myself up and do it all again. I had nothing, and yet I had everything. The life I'd left behind was nothing but a distant memory.

Work progressed slowly on the bionic fabric as each thread was painstakingly woven together by hand. After eight months and 26 previous failed attempts, I was convinced that this was the one. The dining table was covered in wires and electronics, all converging into a heavily modified control system salvaged from an old golf buggy. I held my breath as my finger hovered over the 'on' button. Click! The all too familiar hum of electricity pulsed through the fabric as it lay there, defying all commands to move. So, I did what any good scientist would do; I cranked up the power. Smoke began to billow from the fabric as I fumbled through the nest of wires for the 'off' switch. Click! The fabric was now truly dead. *Oh well, what have I got to lose?* thought as I carefully poured my precious bionic blood over the remains of the bionic fabric. "One last time, let's see what you've got left in you." I said aloud as I returned the empty bottle of bionic blood to the table and lazily pressed the 'on' switch. To my amazement, it came to life. It moved! I turned it off, then back on, and again it moved. I burst into tears as I tried to process what had just happened. My design had finally come to life. I stayed there frozen for some time before I was able to pick up the phone and call Viv. We shared that brief but beautiful moment together, talking about all things possible.

Days turned into weeks and months as my research continued down this new path. In time I had a visitor from next door. "Hi! I'm Darcy from next door. Cool crib! Can I come in?" The back door to the beach house was a roller door, and it always remained open. "Sure, my name's Andrew. Welcome." Hat on sideways, Darcy 'slid on in' with all the finesse of the coolest kid in school. "Shoes off, please!" I said. "I like to respect this space." He did so and started wandering around with an attitude of 'Yeh; I dig it!' After a while, he said, "Blimey, are you a genius or something'! Ya know how to use all this stuff?" "Yes, it's pretty easy when you know how. But hey, there's something I'd like to show you first." I opened what appeared to be a secret door to him. Eyes wide, he could not believe what he was seeing: a climate-controlled room full of 3D printers, all working feverishly like busy little bees. I heard him mutter a few exclamatory swear words under his breath as he walked into the room. "Oh my god! I cannot believe that you have these. We have one at school, but it's so slow and always booked out." "Well, if you'd like to learn, I'd be happy to teach you. I need a lab assistant. Would you be interested?" "Fuck, yeh!" was his reply. We chatted for a bit as I started to introduce him to the rest of the lab – until his mother called him for dinner. "You'd better go. And make sure you get permission from your mum every time you come over!"

The next day, Darcy brought his friend Jamie. Jamie looked at Darcy strangely when he took off his shoes but shrugged his shoulders and did the same. Darcy could not hold back his excitement and said, "Hey, Fuckwit, check this out." This did not sit well with me, so I called them both over and said, "Under this roof, there is only one rule, and that is to use the word 'sir' or 'ma'am' after a person's name. Let me show you. "Jamie, sir. Check this out."" I could tell that they thought it was a stupid rule, but I asked them to try it anyway. Jokingly, they tried it, and within minutes their attitude changed. It was almost as if every time they said 'sir', they were both giving and receiving respect.

The 'sir' word seemed to be doing the job. I sat quietly in my research, watching every now and again how they self-transformed. It wasn't long before they started asking, "Andrew, sir, what's this machine for?" I replied, "What do you think? Guess!" And so the games began. The respect they now had for each other helped a lot, allowing them to explore safely without fear of humiliation. It was beautiful to watch and the perfect time to introduce inspiration. I could see that they were curious about everything in the lab. There was an entire wall of specialised lab equipment, rows and rows of chemicals, electronic components and equipment, and an endless array of engineering tools. There were whiteboards everywhere, allowing the freedom to explore ideas without much commitment or effort. I chose one of the smaller whiteboards and drew a line down the middle. On the left, I wrote some of the tasks that needed to be done around the lab by a lab assistant and on the right, a list of 'thank you projects' carefully constructed to secretly inspire their current schoolwork and maybe a little bit more.

"When a lab assistant completes a task on the left," I explained to them, "their reward is that they get to choose a fully funded thank-you project from the right. Now, Darcy, can you do a hardware upgrade on all the 3D printers in the print room?" "I dunno, suppose!" which was his way of saying, "Yes, absolutely." After a week's solid effort, Darcy and Jamie, along with a few friends, finally finished the task, so I asked them to demonstrate how they did it. To my surprise, they rattled off a list of advanced engineering concepts that are unique to 3D printing, showing why they needed to deviate from some of the website's instructions. Satisfied with their efforts, I scratched off the 'upgrade 3D printers' task from the left of the whiteboard and offered them the choice of a thank-you project from the right. Running over with excitement, they pretended to discuss an already agreed project, then turned to me and said in one voice, "We want to build an HHO generator, please!"

This little beast is not something to be messed with, and to build one from scratch would require some pretty serious chemistry and physics knowledge. But they were kids and wanted the power to cut through anything like butter. "You know the drill. You need to get your parent's permission to be here. And you need your parent's permission to build any of these projects. This is really dangerous stuff if you don't know what you are doing!" Soon enough, I had their parents at my door. At first, I thought it was a rioting mob, but quickly realised that they were angry because they were not invited. "Maybe next time. They've earned this one, and you'll have to do the same. No exceptions." The look on Darcy's and Jamie's faces was priceless. For the first time, they had power over their parents.

Little did they know that they had just taken their first step in becoming a Wholehearted Leader, just like I did all those years ago. And little did I know of the devastation about to be unleashed on me.

Progress on the bionics research was going very well. Partnerships were formed with leading universities in the field of self-organising nanoparticles, enabling this technology to literally build itself at the atomic level. This really excited me as now it opened up the possibility of creating bionic fabric cheaply, making this technology available to everyone. And for people like Viv, using the fabric to create bionic pants that are soft to the touch, worn under their clothes, and walks for them was ground-breaking. It also showed the potential to perfectly replicate a human heart with a bit more research. (Now, if that's not wholeheartedness, I don't know what is!)

But life had another curveball waiting. The spike in the company's spending caught the attention of the ATO, resulting in the company being audited. At the time, I was not worried because we were expecting this and had spent the previous four months getting our accountants prepared. However, the company's six-month contingency plan for the audit process collapsed around the nine-month mark, definitely no match for the 18 months that the audit actually took. Devastated, I had no choice but to let all 40+ staff and researchers go and close the doors. Such valuable technology lost.

I had nothing, no money, living off cabbage and coconuts and the grace of my parents, no marriage, and a destroyed reputation. My thoughts went dark, engulfing me with no sight of reprieve. The pain was intense. My entire self-worth was built on respect and trust, and now I had neither. It felt like I had done wrong to everyone I had ever loved. I completely believed that the only option was to end it, twice.

And it was during that moment, that 'Come to Jesus' moment, lying there emotionally bare, that I saw the only thing I was not willing to let go of, my core belief ... 'To do the right thing at the right time with the right people, no matter the pain.'

At that moment, I was nothing but that core belief. I lived it. I breathed it. I was it.

And it cut through that pain. Not knowing my path, I slowly took one small step, then another, and another until I dragged myself out of that dark place. The ATO audit played an important role in one of my biggest and most important life lessons. It provided one of the few mechanisms strong enough to strip away all my hardened layers of ego, allowing me to get the tiniest glimpse of why I am: to be wholehearted. And for that, I am forever grateful.

So, do the work. Pain is your friend. Pain will push you off balance emotionally, allowing you to see yourself from a different angle and giving you the opportunity to grow. Trust me; it's worth it. Wholehearted leadership is not a 'thing' that you can learn in a classroom or book or even reading these words. The potential of wholeheartedness is innate in all of us, and it emerges when you truly ask for it, push for it, and want it more than anything else. And for the rest of us, it is unknowingly thrust upon us.

At the time of writing this, the ATO case is still ongoing. Sadly, Viv died three days ago, leaving me forever unable to complete my promise to him. But every one of my life experiences has helped me shine through some version of wholeheartedness. And I believe that my life has been shining brightly all my life, accepting every life gift earned along the way.

For me, living life is now the intentional act of every moment:

1. Accepting my inner demons. They've made me strong.
2. Quietening the noise in my head. It's a distraction.
3. Listening from my heart. That's where magic happens.

And having more loving conversations at work and at home by …

only making statements about myself, and
only asking questions to the other person.

These quotes from Marianne Williamson sum it up beautifully…

Our deepest fear is not that we are inadequate.
Our deepest fear is that we are powerful beyond measure.
It is our light, not our darkness
That most frightens us.

Your playing small
Does not serve the world.
There's nothing enlightened about shrinking
So that other people won't feel insecure around you.

We are all meant to shine,

As children do.

ABOUT THE AUTHOR
Andrew Lizzio

Andrew is a somewhat quiet, unassuming and understated person. He hates crowds but loves people. Fears conflict but values differences. And believes that nature is a wonderful teacher if we dare to truly listen.

If you were to ask Andrew to label himself, he would proudly say 'a geek'. He wrote his first computer program at the age of five, graduated from university as a computer scientist, and spent the last 30 years designing computer systems for small and large organisations. But what makes Andrew different is his ability to design systems that somehow design themselves. That is systems that self-adapt to be more relevant to the people that use them while they are using them.

Andrew has two small start-up companies: Wizup, currently developing a world-first application for all schools and universities that accurately assesses a student's true understanding of any content while they are learning it, making student exams and teacher administration a thing of the past. And Clarus which has just secured a worldwide patent on bionic technology to help paraplegics walk again. The culture of both companies is based on a deep belief that, given the right environment, passionate individuals working together will make a difference and maybe even change the world.

But for Andrew, changing the world is coincidental. His focus is on the journey itself, building the courage to take the next imperfect step, daring to truly listen, and learning how to shine brightly.

CONNECT WITH ANDREW

LinkedIn: *www.linkedin.com/in/andrew-lizzio*

NICKY MIH
A Book, A Promise And A Mission Of Epic Proportions

I never read much before I was eleven. I loved school and always did very well – I just never read. At 11, my teacher told my mum I had to read for 20 minutes every day, so Mum allowed me the quiet of her bedroom away from my brothers and sister and the noise of the TV.

The first evening I didn't even open my book; I looked at Mum's ornaments on her dresser and the intricate carving on the wardrobe and gazed out of the window. On the second evening, I pulled the photo albums out of the wardrobe and looked through those. On the third evening, I decided I may as well open my book and give this reading thing a go.

Within two weeks, I loved reading. I loved the characters. I loved the adventures. I loved getting lost between the pages of someone else's life. Before long, I didn't need the privacy of Mum's room; I would sit on the couch among my family, TV on, and be completely absorbed in my book.

I read every book in my school library. I joined the local library and read every book in there. My favourites were the *Choose Your Own Adventure* books. I read and re-read every one of them to find out what would have happened at each turning point if I had made a different decision.

I read my way through five libraries. By 15, I was reading books like *A Woman in Her Own Right* and *Feel the Fear and Do It Anyway*.

Then I read a bunch of books that upset me massively yet inspired me greatly. From Mukhtar in Pakistan, who was sentenced to a gang rape as punishment for a crime her brother allegedly committed to ten-year-old Nujood in Yemen, who walked into a courtroom and requested they help her get divorced.

I hated that such awful things happen.
I wanted to help.
But I didn't know how.

So after reading each book, I placed it carefully back on my bookshelf and went about my life as usual.

But I couldn't keep reading these books and doing nothing! So I made a promise: *the next book I read, no matter what the country or what the issue, I won't just put it back on the shelf. I'll do something.*

The next book I read was about sex trafficking in Cambodia.

The author said she was tired and needed help. There it was: the way forward I'd been looking for, the opportunity to follow through on my promise to do something.

I sent five emails but didn't hear back. So I went about my life as usual, again. 18 months passed.

And then, studying for a Diploma in Coaching, I was asked three questions that stopped me in my tracks:

1. *What is it that you've always wanted to do but haven't done yet?*
2. *In what ways are you not sharing the best of you with the world?*
3. *Where have you not stepped up yet?*

What came up for me was that I'd not come good on my promise to do something about sex trafficking. I thought of the quote, "All that is necessary for evil to prevail is for good men to do nothing." When I thought of it like this, that these girls are being tortured, electrocuted and raped because good people are doing nothing to stop it, I knew it was time to step up.

I was going to Cambodia!

On the plane, my anxiety grew. What the hell was I doing? I was about to walk into an issue so frickin' immense, it was ridiculous. Who was I kidding? What the heck could I possibly do? This was a stupid idea. I was just one person!

Then I breathed and remembered Susan Jeffers' book, *Feel the Fear and Do It Anyway*.

I spent the next few days observing the work of an anti-trafficking organisation and aftercare centre. We were to go to the homes of a group of sex workers to give them soap and condoms. By doing so each month, we could find out when underage girls came from the countryside to engage in sex work.

I followed the team through alleyways piled with dirt and rubbish, and then we made our way over rickety planks of wood that led out over a lake and created a pathway that connected the houses together. The wood was rotten in many places, with bits of boards missing, and the planks moved unsteadily as I walked tentatively across them. I imagined falling straight through into the dirty, stagnant water below.

The team I was accompanying interrupted my thoughts: "Be ready to run if we have to."

Run? I could barely walk slowly and tentatively!

If they were to yell "run", well, I'd certainly try. But I had visions of them all running and me trying to keep up, clumsily losing my footing and falling into the lake while watching the team speed off in their car.

What the heck was I doing here?

We reached the homes of a group of sex workers. The women rolled out a mat across what floorboards there were, and I tried to position myself so that I wouldn't fall through one of the many holes into that lake below.

We sat in a circle while the pimps stood at the door, controlling how long we could talk and what we could talk about. One woman breastfed her baby as we talked, a small child played beside his mum, and two girls, aged 13 and 14, had, indeed, recently joined the group from the countryside.

When the team had finished their conversation, they turned to me, the visitor, and asked if I had any questions. I did – of course, I did. I had a million thoughts racing through my head. But something stopped me, and I became acutely aware that I had been welcomed into these women's homes, complete with children playing and pimps at the door. Instead, I asked whether they had any questions they'd like to ask me first. They did. And I learnt more from their questions than I ever could have by asking any of my own.

I was a million things as we made our way back to the car: relieved no one had yelled "run", humbled that these women had welcomed me into their home, saddened that there were toddlers breastfeeding and playing and that this was going to be their childhood, stunned that the pimps had let us in, upset that girls of only 13 and 14 had just arrived from the provinces to engage in sex work.

I didn't sleep very well that night.

After a month working with trafficking survivors, I asked them how I could help. I learned that the day they got rescued, the traffickers didn't go without a girl, they just went out to the rural villages and took a new young girl. They said, "Nicky, go out to the rural villages, find the girls who aren't in school and get them into school." I looked around the room. Not one of them had been in school when they were trafficked, and they believed if they had been in school, they would have been safe.

I had no idea they would hand me a mission of such epic proportions, a mission I had no idea how to achieve. I'd never even been to a rural village. I had no idea how to get to one, or what to do when I got there, let alone how to find girls who weren't in school or how to get them into school. But I'd asked the question, and they had answered, and the course of my life had changed in an instant.

They were very clear. And I knew in every cell of my body that they were right.

They had identified a gap. I had thought that I would find an organisation focusing on prevention and I'd be able to help them. But I couldn't find one. What they knew was needed didn't yet exist. There were organisations collaborating with the police on rescue operations, there were aftercare centres, and there were legal teams working in the justice system to bring about prosecutions. But I couldn't find an organisation out in these rural villages specifically identifying these girls before the traffickers did.

So that's what we do. I now lead a team of professionals that includes education officers and social workers. We work with community leaders, local councils, and schools. We've learned which villages traffickers will target and how they identify the most vulnerable when they get there. We prevent school-aged girls being trafficked into the commercial sex industry by addressing the many factors that make them vulnerable to being targeted by traffickers.

When the survivors asked me to find the girls who weren't in school and get them into school, I thought that was my mission in its entirety. Don't get me wrong, I didn't think it would be easy; I had zero idea how I'd even do that much. But we did it. Little did I know, that really was the easy part! They never mentioned keeping them in school and how hard that would be.

The biggest part of our program is our monthly safety visits, social work interventions, and community training. We teach families and their children how to protect themselves from exploitation and abuse. We help families problem-solve. We address complex, ever-changing and often interlinked factors such as poverty, hunger, illness, family violence and breakdown, addiction, unemployment, migration and debt. We provide education and guidance to help the family find their way through it, all the time keeping their daughter's safety and right to education at the forefront. We don't give girls and their families charity; we give them a team.

Six years in, we were securing the safety and education of 700 girls, when one day, things fell apart in a spectacular way.

My Cambodian team demanded that their annual salary increase be double what it was, even though it was already well in excess of the government's requirement.

I value my team and am committed to best practice, including providing a great workplace and remunerating them fairly, so it was very important to get this right. The criteria I used for making this decision were: Is it sustainable? Is it evidence-based? Is it fair?

When I said "no" to the pay increase, I hadn't made the decision lightly.

I'd sat in a room for two days with my Australian staff and worked out how we could give them this huge pay rise. I always want to make sure that being a charity, and never having enough money to secure the safety of all the children we know need to be kept safe, is never a reason to underpay our team. I wanted to make the right decision, and if giving the pay rise was the right thing to do, then I'd say "yes" and it'd be my job to figure out how the heck to deliver on it.

So we sat for two days figuring it out. Then we considered each person's skills, experience and performance, and imagined giving them the requested increase.

And quite simply, they weren't worth that yet. They were still inexperienced and in training. They were at university, studying non-related degrees, and we were teaching them social work skills. The salary level they suggested was that of a university graduate with a social work-related degree, with one or two years of social work experience, who needs little training or supervision in order to complete the requirements of that job.

I did not want to underpay; that was not fair on my team. Likewise, I did not want to overpay, as that is not fair to other organisations. I remembered very clearly a conversation with the director of an organisation back when I first began the program. He implored me not to pay my staff higher than other organisations; this was their biggest challenge, as it resulted in them losing high-quality staff to newly established foreign organisations. So I aimed for fairness on both sides.

A review of job advertisements for similar positions indicated that our salaries were in line with other organisations of similar size and scope. I also contacted a number of organisations, and each opened up their salary scales to me, which also confirmed we were paying appropriately for my team's qualifications and experience.

And so we decided that, while we could increase salaries, we would not.

I was provided with two weeks in which to reconsider their request and "respond positively." In a culture where respect features incredibly highly, I considered this really rude. They would never give a village leader, a commune leader or a school director a timeframe in which to respond to them, nor instruct them to respond favourably. They did not extend that same level of respect to me.

They held the belief we could not run the program without them. They believed that no matter what they asked for, providing they all asked for it, we'd have to oblige, because, otherwise, our program would collapse. They knew we wouldn't want that because we wouldn't want the girls on our program to suffer. They weren't thinking about whether their actions were smart or ethical. They weren't thinking about their loyalty to Free To Shine, or to the girls they worked with. They really didn't think beyond 'if we all stick together, they'll have to give in'. We urged them to look ahead at the consequences.

I think they had learned about collective bargaining and striking. There were several high-profile cases of employers who were exploiting their staff – staff who were on a third of the salary our team were on, who received a fifth of the annual increases our team received. I thought it right for these exploited workers to stand together to demand fair work conditions and fair pay from these corporations so willing to exploit people; I was baffled that our team was applying that to us.

One of the most bizarre things was that the employee studying law, who possibly drove this action along with a couple of other key team members, was not driven by money. I do not believe the salary increase was his motivating factor, though he certainly wasn't motivated by ethics or fair employment either. I think he was simply keen to test out something in the real world that he'd learned in class, to find out if he could bring together his entire group of colleagues and demand change. I'm sure he thought it would work because they knew how much we valued them, and we'd do anything we could for them.

The bit I really didn't like was that they believed that if backed into a corner, we'd have to give in to their demands. They kept telling us we couldn't run the program without them, that we were in Cambodia and we needed them. For them, this social experiment had turned into an 'us and them' scenario.

I don't appreciate being backed into a corner and I don't give up easily. If I was someone looking for an easy life, I would not be tackling sex trafficking in a developing country. No. It got my back up. I'd built this thing. I'd given six years of my life to it. I wasn't scared or worried, upset or emotional; I was calm, clear, and logical. If I gave in to a demand, not because I thought it the right thing to do but simply because I was backed into a corner, then they'd hold all the power, and I'd have to give in to every demand whenever they felt like making one and to whatever it was they felt like demanding. That was no way to run an organisation; that wasn't being a leader – it was being a hostage.

I told them two more weeks to "respond positively" was not required, their requests had already been carefully considered, and there would be no change from the original response. Then things began to unravel, very quickly.

They didn't arrive for work. In came the messages, one after another, claiming they were sick.

Their striking didn't bother us. This is a country where people have been incredibly disenfranchised, their human rights completely abused, and they've had little avenue for recourse. We supported their right to strike; we even taught them how to do it lawfully. My issue was the manner in which they went about it and the dishonesty that they never admitted to it being a strike. They claimed they were, all 15 of them, unexpectedly brought down by illness within 15 minutes of each other.

Completely bizarrely, while on strike, one of them turned up to the office to use one of our computers and the internet to do his university assignment!

I had learned when establishing Free To Shine that a common concern of Australians thinking about donating was the ethics and honesty of Cambodian staff, and it was of paramount importance to me that I could place hand on heart and, with full integrity, tell donors that our staff were completely honest. We had continuously taught and demonstrated that it was completely acceptable to make mistakes, mistakes could be made and openly discussed, but honesty was always required.

And they could talk to us about anything. And they did; from dangerous situations they found themselves in to family and relationship issues – they came to us with everything. Nothing was off-limits and they trusted us to help them. So the striking itself wasn't an issue; it was the lying about it that was.

It meant that from this moment forward, I could not tell donors that I trusted this group of Cambodians implicitly, that they were ethical and honest. And that was a huge problem.

On the third day, all 15 returned to work, smiling and laughing as if nothing had happened. I needed to discuss with them their lack of honesty and its consequences, and I wanted them to carefully consider their choices. I requested each of them attend a meeting with management. They refused. They were to receive written warnings for dishonesty and failure to act professionally and respectfully. They informed us they didn't want their warnings; they'd conduct themselves the way they saw fit, not the way we deemed appropriate. They told us they'd see us on payday, and, with that, they walked out.

One threw insults, and one threw shoes. And they were gone.

We were stunned. What had just happened? We shook our heads, our eyes wide with shock. Had they just resigned even though they hadn't explicitly said so, or were they striking illegally again? By this point, it didn't much matter – they were out of warnings. What the heck? We had just lost a whole team. My next step was to terminate their employment, all 15 of them. And I did.

How Free To Shine survived this is incredible, and I owe oodles of gratitude to Stacy and Beth, our two Australian team members who stuck it out at a time when most people would have run. It was utterly heartbreaking and confusing, a whirlwind. And it wasn't over.

Bizarrely, they offered to come back to work if I fired Beth instead – never mind that she had done nothing wrong. On the contrary, unlike them, she had behaved ethically and with the utmost integrity and a great deal of courage.

At this point, I was offered a way to make it easier: Beth offered to resign so I could take back the Cambodian staff. While that might have avoided the immediate catastrophe, it wasn't the right or best thing to do. Instead, I chose to do what was necessary and handle the consequences.

I received a threat from the employee I believed to be driving this action. It was disgusting. It was in the form of a metaphor, so it was unclear whether he was threatening to kill the organisation, or me, or Beth. What could we do other than not ride on motorbikes, since most hits target people when riding their bikes? My two Australian team members had a difficult decision to make: stay and help us rebuild, or return to the safety of Australia?

They both chose to stay. That's the commitment to the girls and their families that I wish I had seen in our Cambodian staff.

But was the threat directed not at us as individuals, but at Free To Shine? What might the effects be on 700 families if he damaged our organisation? I got angry. The children were on our program because of their unique vulnerability to being targeted by traffickers, and this team had just walked away from them – no notice, no ensuring the program continued, no preserving the children's safety while we recruited new staff.

By this point, I had become really proud of Free To Shine. The organisation was the creation of those young women who had survived the torture of traffickers and rapists; I was just the conduit that had brought their concept into existence so that other girls would not suffer in a similar way. And it had been built properly, on good foundations. It was working really well for 700 families. And one disgruntled law student wanted to kill it off? Yeah, this peeved me.

Our saga had not ended. We were summoned to a meeting at the Department of Labour. The labour inspector knew about the events of the previous two weeks and was to determine whether the team had been unfairly dismissed or not and what the appropriate course of action was from here.

I knew we had to remain truthful, continue to make good ethical decisions, and that we would come through it, albeit dishevelled. We could have crumbled and cried. We could have run home to Australia. But we made it through. The labour inspector determined we were right to terminate, asked me to rebuild, and assured me of his support with employees in the future.

We seized the opportunity to restructure, strengthen and improve. We had a clean slate, and we were determined to make the absolute best of it. We ascertained what changes we wanted to make to our program, policies and procedures now that we didn't have any employees to resist change. We would get our program up and running, we'd do it quickly and we'd make sure we were even better than before.

Then the phone calls started coming in from various ex-team members asking for their jobs back. We told them they were too late, and we set about figuring out specifically what qualities we wanted in our new team.

Further phone calls came in the next week from the former team, "X girl in Y village needs to be followed up about Z issue. I know we did a bad thing, please don't let the girls suffer because of our choices." We thanked them for letting us know and assured them we'd follow it up. It seemed they did care about the girls. They really did get swept up in those efforts to secure a high pay rise, with insufficient thought to ethics or consequences.

Sometimes I can't believe that we are still standing, completely rebuilt, and so much stronger for it. We did it! We did it for the girls and their families, who deserve someone to come through for them when everyone else bails.

Now we have a new Cambodian team; an older, wiser, more experienced and more educated team. We now have qualified and experienced social workers as well as education officers. Our program was only down for two months and operating on bare bones for a further two. The fact is we lost 59 girls through this: two of whom we have never been able to locate nor ascertain what happened to them. That breaks my heart and makes me mad. It also proves, if ever I doubt it, the necessity of our program. Most of the 59 girls we lost during these four months were found, through the extensive efforts and follow-up work of our new social workers. It took almost a year to find some of them and ascertain their safety. Many have now returned to their villages and to our program and the safety of school.

I don't think we'll ever understand what happened or why. We were tired, hurt and confused, but we handled it. And we're stronger for it.

I'm going to finish my chapter with a quote from Alfred Adler, "Follow your heart but take your brain with you."

Wholehearted Leadership is calm, quiet and strong. It requires integrity, courage, and understanding. It means being authentic. Wholehearted Leadership is leading with your whole heart. But what's the alternative? If you don't do something with your whole heart, are you doing something half-heartedly – just half-assing it? What's the point of that? Why even bother? Wholehearted Leadership is about leading something worthy of your time and effort; something that matters enough to warrant doing, and doing properly.

The way you lead is a reflection of the way you live. Wholehearted Leadership, in my opinion, starts with wholehearted living.

ABOUT THE AUTHOR
Nicky Mih

Nicky Mih is a woman who makes things happen. She believes in our capacity to live and lead differently. With a background in psychology, teaching and coaching, she's on a mission to prevent children being trafficked into the commercial sex industry, a mission set for her by survivors themselves.

Nicky is the co-founder and Managing Director of Free To Shine, a child protection organisation preventing children being trafficked into the commercial sex industry in Cambodia. Nicky leads a team of professionals that includes education officers and social workers. They work with community leaders, local councils, schools and families to prevent girls being trafficked and help them achieve their rights to access education, safe drinking water, enough food and adequate shelter.

Nicky is the author of Do What Matters, an Amazon #1 bestselling book. Do What Matters is a book about courage and achieving the seemingly impossible. It is for people who are ready to step up in their life and leadership. Nicky speaks at conferences around the world, sharing the lessons she's learned, resonating with people and organisations globally. Through her lessons in leadership, business and life, Nicky has a lasting impact on the way people choose to live, work and do business.

CONNECT WITH NICKY

Website: *www.freetoshine.org*
LinkedIn: *www.linkedin.com/in/nickymih*
Facebook: *www.facebook.com/FreeToShine.org*
Do What Matters Book: *www.freetoshine.org/dowhatmatters*

SARAH-JANE PETER-SCHLINGMANN

Stepping Into My Power; Leading With Heart

I loaded my bicycle and a duffle bag of belongings into the bus and climbed on board. Along with $600, everything I owned was on that bus as I drove away from my little hometown, aged 18. I had been fascinated by technology for as long as I could remember, so moving to the big city seemed like the only way I could make my dream of working in tech a reality. But it was tough for me as a fresh-faced graduate with little experience. I just couldn't seem to land any job in tech. So, I gave up on my dream, and instead I worked in the property sector.

One day, I met a handsome young man. He swept me off my feet in a whirlwind romance and asked me to quit my job so we could travel the world. I quit my job, but I didn't end up travelling. Instead, just six months after we had met, I found myself pregnant, married and unemployed. It was at that time that I started helping small businesses with their websites.

Those early days of consulting were filled with fear and uncertainty. I remember that first meeting with a client. They asked, "Can you come and meet with us tomorrow morning?"

I woke up and rummaged through my closet but, because I hadn't worked for a few months and was now pregnant, none of my business clothes fit. My initial thought was, *I can't go. I need to cancel. I can't do this.* But I didn't cancel. Instead, I put on a ridiculous short, bright-red dress and off I went.

When I walked into that meeting, I was so nervous my hands were shaking. I didn't look professional, and I wasn't sure if my technical skills were good enough for the client. To my surprise, the two women I met with that day were not at all put off by my dress and pregnant belly. In fact, they were extremely relieved to have found someone like me to help them. We ended up working together for 12 years.

So, the first step on my entrepreneurial journey was simply to show up in the first place. Every time I was terrified and thought I might not be able to do something, I just showed up and kept trying. I did this enough times that I started to prove to myself that most of those barriers in my way had been created in my own mind. I got in the habit of walking right up to those barriers and stepping on through.

However, being a highly capable and increasingly confident entrepreneur didn't guarantee that I would have an easy ride in life. Things were not good for me at home. My happy-ever-after fairytale was not so happy after all.

Domestic violence is the sort of thing that happens to other people. Not to me. That's what I thought. I kept telling myself that my situation wasn't so bad, but I packed a bag and kept it in my closet just in case. I drew a line in the sand. I told myself that if it happened again, I would take that suitcase, take my baby and I would leave. So that's how I found myself shivering in the cold rain with a baby in my arms, wondering how I was going to get food and if I would find a place for us to sleep that night. My idea of homelessness was that we would find a homeless shelter; surely people wouldn't let a mother and baby sleep out in the cold. I sat with social workers as they called shelter after shelter, and my heart sank as each one informed us that they were full for the night. I had hit rock bottom.

Thankfully, the social workers that were with me didn't give up. A mix of gratitude and shame flooded me as I accepted food and clothing from the Salvation Army. The plastic shopping bag of frozen food felt cold pressed against my leg as I juggled a warm baby, a pram and the suitcase on the three-hour bus trip to find a bed for the night. A depth of sadness washed over me as we bumped and bounced along that winding road. Tears rolled down my cheeks, hidden in the darkness of the dimly lit bus as my baby slept peacefully against my chest. I knew that I never wanted to be in that situation ever again.

A few years later, when things had settled down, my business was starting to grow. I had taken on a few team members and things were looking good. Still, as a woman in tech, I faced challenges and obstacles that my male counterparts never did. I was often the only woman in the room and several times I delivered key presentations or negotiated business deals while pregnant or while having a miscarriage.

One time when I was pregnant with my second child, I was negotiating a deal with a room full of men. One of them suddenly shouted, "What the hell! I can see it moving!" and pointed at my stomach. Everyone stared at my belly as it wobbled and jerked around. He then asked if we should stop the negotiations and pick them up at a better time. I looked him in the eye and asked, "When would be a better time?" There was an awkward silence until thankfully one of the guys said, "Let's just press on."

I raced out of that meeting knowing that I would probably be late for my next appointment, the Mother's Day morning tea at kindergarten. By the time I arrived the doors to the kindergarten hall were closed and locked. I circled the building, trying every door to no avail. Then I found a roller door that was open just a tiny bit. There I was, heavily pregnant, crawling under a roller door on hands and knees in front of all the staff and parents. By the time I found my daughter I was only five minutes late, but she was already in tears. I landed a million-dollar deal that day, but the cost of the deal was a broken heart.

I made a decision. I knew that devoting time and attention to my children would reduce my ability to successfully grow my business, but it was a sacrifice I was willing to make. I would find a way to be financially secure, but not at the cost of compromising my relationship with my children.

I ran my business remotely so I could be close to my kids. I brought on my first few team members, one was physically disabled, and another was a parent of young children. So, it made sense to continue running remotely. In a post-COVID world, that seems like an ordinary thing to do. At the time, it was a revolutionary idea.

This concept often left people confused or thinking that my business wasn't legitimate because we didn't have an office. They would often ask, "How do you know if people are working?" and I would ask them the same question back. I would try to explain that perhaps they themselves should consider remote working within their own organisations and almost everyone responded that they wished they could, but it just wouldn't be possible.

Many times, I felt uncertain about my unusual choice to run a remote team. I knew that there was a possibility that my team was working less efficiently or taking advantage of me without me knowing it. But there were moments that made me feel that it didn't matter. Seeing one of my team members taking the weekly meeting remotely with one baby in a baby carrier on his chest and his other baby on a baby carrier on his back, I believed that those babies would grow up to be happier, healthier and have a better relationship with their father. No matter how much I thought about it, that seemed worthwhile, even if it meant a risk of reduced profit for me.

I knew my business wasn't growing as fast or as profitably as others, but why do businesses have to grow quickly and make a lot of profit anyway? How much is enough? I didn't see the need for relentless, ruthless growth if it came at a high cost, especially if that cost was not financial, but rather something as intangible as a child's relationship with their parent. I just couldn't understand why other people couldn't see it the same way.

Being a visionary can be frustrating. When you can clearly imagine a path to a better future, being met with resistance, disbelief or even outright ridicule from others can be deflating. As a young entrepreneur, I often responded to this negativity from others as evidence that my vision was fundamentally flawed. I gave up on ideas and missed opportunities. As years went by, I saw many of those same ideas brought to life by others. Sometimes the same people who rejected my vision would return to me years later proposing my original idea. It dawned on me that my vision wasn't the problem. It was my failure to bring others along on the journey. But I also learned to be resilient in my vision, because some people will never be ready or capable to understand. Some people will discount your vision, just because it comes from you.

One time, I walked into a luncheon, sat down in my seat, and before I could say a word, a high-ranking government executive pointed his finger at me. "We don't need young people like you to tell us how to innovate," he said. "We need grey-haired men with experience in business." Almost everyone at the table laughed. At age 34, my competence and value had been judged based on my appearance.

The man sitting beside me turned to me and said, "Well, he clearly knows nothing about innovation!" The two of us then had a fascinating discussion about innovation and future technologies. Our discussion was interrupted as the MC announced our keynote for the day. The man I had been speaking to stood up and walked onto the stage to deliver the keynote. He was a globally renowned tech innovator from California.

The contrast between how these two men had treated me was an inspirational moment. I knew which person I would rather be. Sitting there, knowing how much value I could have delivered if I had been given a voice, I committed myself to always approach others with curiosity and respect. I decided I would listen to and elevate the voices of people who might otherwise be overlooked. Most importantly, the absurdity of the government executive's comments helped me to learn to stop seeking validation from everyone, and instead have faith in what I knew to be true, even if others couldn't see it.

I had a lofty goal of achieving financial freedom, aiming for excellence in business, being a model parent and providing flexibility to my employees, and I was making it work. When I had my second child, the business had grown large enough that I was able to take maternity leave. Everything was going well, but then suddenly it all fell apart.

We were developing a website for an airline. It had a tight timeline, but with all three of my team members working on it, we would have scraped by okay. Then, right in the middle of the project, one of my three employees resigned without notice. Another employee went on honeymoon and the third took time off for university. So, there I was, breastfeeding around the clock and coding a web application mostly on my own.

With just a few hours of sleep each night I was getting very stressed. I would spend the day looking after my baby and getting my daughter to school. If I was lucky, I would get a few hours' programming and responding to clients while my son was asleep during the day. Each night I cooked dinner and tucked the kids into bed then started programming. I programmed until I couldn't see anymore, usually around two a.m., gave the bub another breastfeed, crashed into bed exhausted, woke up for breastfeeding in the night and then dragged myself out of bed at dawn to do it all over again.

One Sunday afternoon, the day before the project was due, my husband said, "You need to stop coding and take a break!" So I walked outside with my mind absolutely buzzing with code and all the things I needed to do. I took a deep breath ... and let it all go.

I was getting very Zen, trimming some bamboo hedges, and trying my best not to think about the project. I looked around at the golden afternoon sunlight bouncing off the leaves. I felt the warm breeze on my cheek, and I listened as the birds called sweetly from the trees. I reached down to pick up a bamboo branch, and suddenly a snake jumped out and bit me on the leg. I looked down and I thought, *I don't have time for this!* I inspected the bite marks on my leg, thinking to myself, *If I tell anyone about this, I'll end up in hospital, and that project isn't going to be delivered on time.*

So I didn't tell anyone that I had been bitten by a snake. I cooked dinner, tucked the kids into bed, sat down at my computer and programmed until two a.m. The next morning when I woke up my head was pounding. I could barely walk straight. I got my daughter ready for school. I put the baby to bed and delivered the project on time.

A couple of days later, and after a few good nights of sleep, fluid started oozing out of the snake bite on my leg. That is when I realised what I had done. I had risked my life to deliver a project. Looking back, the mistake I made was not that I hadn't told anyone about the snake bite. The problem was that I had gotten myself into a state where I was so sleep deprived and stressed that I was unable to make smart choices.

It highlighted to me that physical and mental health is fundamental and must be prioritised above everything. No financial reward or career achievement is worth risking your life, or anyone else's. I took this learning into how I approached management of my team, vowing to myself that I would put the health of my team members and myself first.

My challenges in life taught me that most of us are merely human, struggling with circumstances that unavoidably impact our success at work. I wanted to create a workplace where being human was acceptable. Where people could safely talk about what was really going on and engage in a way that worked for them and their families. I knew that I wanted to do this, even if it meant hampering growth and profitability of the business.

Despite this approach, my business continued to grow. Before too long, we were turning over multimillion-dollar revenues and had secured an impressive list of high-calibre clients, including airlines, software companies and all levels of government.

Before I started my tech company, I had no experience as a leader. I was an executive assistant, and I had never led a team or organisation. I had no idea what I was doing. In some ways, this was a benefit. I didn't know that people expected leaders to be tough, authoritative and unforgiving. Instead, I approached leadership in the way that I believed it should be done, with kindness, empathy and love.

Over time, I started to find that the impact of this was not just higher-than-average employee retention, but something more. When I asked employees why they stayed with my company, they often told me it was because of the culture. I wondered what that meant. What exactly is culture? More importantly, how could we ensure that we kept this culture in place as we grew? So, I started to ask more questions.

I did an exercise where I asked whom we would send to Mars as a representative of our company values. I then started noting down the words that people used when talking about that team member. To my surprise, the word most used was 'passion'. We started talking about our values more and, over time, we articulated these using an acrostic of the company name.

Identifying our values unlocked something powerful for our organisation. It created a clear framework to evaluate the behaviours of ourselves and others.

We had articulated what was most important to us, what defined us as a team, and we were proud of those values.

When we articulated the unspoken truths about how we operated as a team, our defined core values highlighted a culture of authenticity, vulnerability, integrity, empathy and passion. The magic that we felt each day was in knowing that our team members were each contributing what they could in their own way with good intentions. So, when mistakes or problems occurred the conversation was not about assigning blame, it was about identifying how we could fix things as a team and move forward successfully. People were free to share opinions, admit mistakes or ask for help without fear of negative repercussions. We had inadvertently created a workplace culture that put psychological safety at its heart. The result was that we empowered people to thrive.

In my organisation, we are not afraid to talk about weaknesses and challenges. We are all different, and we all bring different strengths to the table. Some of us are great coders, and not so good at communication. Others are excellent communicators and don't know how to code. We don't need everyone to be perfect in every area. We just need them to do what they do well and be supported by a team that can make up the gaps.

For example, one of my team members is autistic and non-verbal. He is also a genius. When we ran data analysis on our developers, we found out that he is the most productive and profitable person on the team, and by a huge margin. When we have a complex coding problem to solve, he's the one the team turns to. He is our superhero. He doesn't speak, and that's okay. Communicating in spoken language is irrelevant to being a good coder, if you have a supportive team working as a unified whole. I believe that when employees are given the tools, freedom, and support to succeed, they can unleash their full potential as unique individuals.

I believe that by showing up myself as an authentic, vulnerable, flawed human being, I helped to foster an environment where people in turn could show up as their true selves, support one another with kindness, and create a culture of trust, respect and belonging.

I have achieved a lot of successful results with my business, including winning international awards. But nothing felt quite so good as hearing my non-verbal team member speak to me for the first time at one of our work parties, seeing his smile, hearing him laugh, getting a great big bear hug from him, and watching him dance with his arms around the shoulders of his teammates. To us he really is a superstar, and I'm glad he knows that. To me that is success.

I believe that our culture has underpinned our performance in business. Having psychological safety at work has created a sense of empowerment and growth for the team that has allowed us to take on seemingly impossible situations.

I've always been fascinated by people who do impossible things. The quadriplegic man who works as a doctor in the emergency room, or the man who climbed Mount Everest with prosthetic legs. People like these know the difference between something that is truly impossible, and something that is just incredibly difficult.

In the same way that we often put imaginary barriers in our own way as individuals, sometimes we do this as a group. Not too long ago, it was believed that running 100 metres in under ten seconds was impossible. During the 1960s several athletes proved this idea wrong, breaking through barriers imposed on them by society's beliefs about what is achievable. Now, world-class sprinters often dip below that magical ten-second mark, that just a few decades ago seemed out of reach.

As a leader, it's important to understand the power of reframing challenges as difficult rather than impossible, and to be frank about the reality of the situation. Building up a track record of listening and responding to your team, and getting through challenging situations together, will establish faith in your leadership even when team members have doubts.

During the COVID-19 pandemic, one of our airline customers collapsed. They owed us hundreds of thousands of dollars in unpaid invoices that were never paid. With several customers similarly impacted, projects cancelled overnight, and lockdowns in effect, my team was very anxious. The financial situation looked bleak, and I wasn't sure how we would make it through. I could have made staff redundant to reduce ongoing costs, but I cared deeply for my team, and leaving any one of them without a job during a pandemic was unthinkable. Instead, I took the problem to my team.

I transparently and honestly told them the brutal truth of the situation. I shared my vision that we would find a way to come through together, but I also told them that I didn't know how we would get there. I was very clear that it was going to be difficult, but I believed it was possible. We needed a plan for survival, so I asked how we could approach it together. I told them that I was reducing my salary, and every single team member volunteered to do the same to help ensure no one would lose their job. After just two weeks at reduced rates, we had turned the business around and were able to confidently restore everyone's salaries.

The day that I was certain we wouldn't need to let anyone go, I broke down in tears of relief. I'm so proud of how we came through that crisis together. Their willingness to make a sacrifice for their fellow team members, and to take on a seemingly impossible situation left an indelible mark on my heart. I feel forever honoured and humbled to have led such a team of loyal and truly good people.

Looking back on my journey, I am thankful for the experiences that have crafted me into the Wholehearted Leader that I am today. There have been stressful times and tears, but also laughter and triumph. I have faced situations that seemed insurmountable and made lots of mistakes, but I persevered.

My experiences taught me to be sensitive to the hidden challenges of people's lives. Now I see the woman standing on the street with a suitcase in her hand and know she needs help. I recognise the look of the First Nation entrepreneur standing in a room full of white fellas in suits, and my heart cries out, "You do belong here!" My experiences have brought me wisdom and empathy and I am grateful for that.

It takes courage to follow your heart and do what you believe is right in the face of adversity and doubt. You must embrace your unique, imperfect self. Celebrate your strengths and acknowledge your weaknesses. Lead with your heart, your intuition and your values, empowering others to be their best selves and creating a culture of trust, respect and collaboration. Lead by example, by caring, by listening and by serving. By stepping into your power and allowing yourself to challenge the status quo you can open up possibilities for change that make a meaningful difference in the world. Have faith that even if it is not always easy, it is a journey worth taking.

ABOUT THE AUTHOR
Sarah-Jane Peterschlingmann

Sarah-Jane Peterschlingmann is the Managing Director and owner of ATech, an award-winning technology company that delivers mission-critical websites for large corporations and governments. Starting as a web developer, she helped to grow ATech from humble beginnings to multimillion-dollar revenues, and has won numerous awards, including International Website of the Year.

Sarah-Jane is an investor, entrepreneur, author, business adviser and technology enthusiast who regularly speaks on the topics of technology, innovation and leadership, and is passionate about empowering others to find the best within themselves.

She has a degree in Information Technology specialising in Digital Electronics and Machine Learning as well as two master's degrees in Business and Investment.

Sarah-Jane is a single parent who lives in Brisbane, Australia. In her spare time, she enjoys being adventurous and keeping active by dancing, hiking, rock climbing and travelling.

CONNECT WITH SARAH-JANE

Website: *www.peterschlingmann.au*

LinkedIn: *www.linkedin.com/in/speterschlingmann*
Instagram: *www.instagram.com/speterschlingmann*

JOHN SMILEK
Values In Leadership And Life

If you've been around a bit, you would have realised that we all have a unique ability, talent or gift, a special feature that makes each of us distinct – some might even consider it a superpower.

You might have read or seen a YouTube video of someone creating amazing works of art from memory, like Stephen Wiltshire, who began creating highly detailed sketches of London landmarks when he was only five. Stephen has since become famous for his "mental snapshots" – his ability to look at a cityscape once, then recreate it in near-perfect detail, drawing and painting panoramas of cities all over the world.

Then there's Terence Tao, a mathematics genius who earned a bachelor's degree, a master's, then a Ph.D. in mathematics from Princeton University by the age of 21. There's also Alma Deutscher, a British composer, pianist and violinist born in 2005. She began playing the piano at the age of two. By six, she had composed her first piano sonata. She has since composed an opera, a violin concerto and several other pieces that have been performed by orchestras around the world.

These are not the typical abilities that we find in society, and it's not an exaggeration to call these superpowers. These are unique traits and abilities that are part of a wide-ranging autistic spectrum and are very apparent.

For others, unique traits are not so obvious. Most of us cannot draw panoramas from memory, solve incredibly complex equations or write a piano sonata, but I have observed abilities, talent and genius in the most inconspicuous places. In fact, I have yet to meet someone who does not possess some unique trait.

Like everyone, people with Asperger's syndrome – affectionately known as Aspies – have strengths and weaknesses. We are often emotionally detached. We see the world through a set of structures and patterns, a way of seeing more akin to the random colours of a Rubik's cube that is aching to be solved. Many engineers, scientists and technicians are on the neuro-diverse spectrum. These people can focus intensely on one specific job, often without having emotions impede their task and sometimes to the exclusion of other interests.

This allows Aspies like me to see the world through a unique framework that is more logical and analytical, weighing up various perspectives while seeing the subtle patterns all around us that many observers miss. One of the most famous people today with Asperger's is Elon Musk. His pattern recognition capabilities are exceptional, which has helped him innovate several industries.

As I travel and meet people, diverse groups and communities, sometimes as a speaker, instructor or team leader, my Aspie quirkiness occasionally pops out. It's always there, but is usually controlled by years of training and constant awareness that I still have much to learn about discerning social cues and body language.

My everyday routine feels much like heading off to school. From the moment I wake to the time I go to bed, I am constantly learning how to navigate the intricate nuances of social interactions, emotions and the complexities of dealing with people.

The hard-wiring doesn't change, but over time I have learned to build alternative routes to reach the same destination. If the fastest route is the highway of thoughts that lead to a social accident, then it might be better to take the off-ramp and try the scenic route, take my time and arrive in a better state of mind, better prepared and avoiding that social head-on. If I don't know where the off-ramp is or if there is none, then I take the time to build one, one experience, one social interaction, one step or misstep at a time, until it becomes the path I not only prefer but often enjoy.

Easy? It is not. It's really hard – damn hard. It takes years, sometimes decades, but the rewards for me have been great, including increased social awareness and the ability to interact comfortably with others. It's interesting that those who know me, at least casually, would find it hard to believe that I'm an Aspie. At least on the surface it's not that obvious, especially as someone often seen effortlessly connecting with diverse groups of people.

Listening to My Community

When my family migrated to Australia, with nothing more than two suitcases, as anyone who's been there knows, it was tough. Although money was always tight and possessions few, I can't remember a time when I didn't see my parents – particularly my mother – helping out new families in need who also came with nothing, escaping communism or war, all wide-eyed and lost in a foreign land.

As a child, I didn't think about the sacrifice it takes to serve others when you yourself have little to give. But what Mum couldn't give in money or material worth, she would give in time and understanding. She spent time having a cup of tea, listening to a young mother's worries and alleviating her fears in this new, strange land, giving counsel and hope that things will be okay. She would often take a plate of sandwiches, bake a cake, find some hand-me-down clothes for the kids, then chat and listen, giving a little advice, always with a smile and another sip of tea.

How does one do this when you're exhausted from work, cleaning and cooking, taking care of life's bits and pieces, and with a young child? But every now and then, off she went to meet a new family at the local immigration centre, giving a little more of her time and friendship.

We eventually settled, living close to a healthy population of immigrants, which gave me the opportunity to pick up a second language before starting primary school, where I was finally introduced to English. As I visited the homes of my friends, I would often overhear their parents' conversations, things that children should never hear. Not being aware that I now understood them gave me exclusive and often covert access to this grown-up world, and I began comparing the values of the different families.

I started to notice a pattern. Despite some families being of the same ethnicity and religion, living in the same area and attending the same church, not every family shared the same values. Like a kid with a new toy, observing people became a fascination. I was captivated.

Over time — as the size of houses grew, the cars became more luxurious, the clothes lavish and some people now in positions of power, such as supervisor, manager or a boss — how the talk changed. Now I overheard some of these people talking themselves up, constantly comparing themselves to their friends and family. I even overheard them putting down my parents, who lived modestly within their means. Would you believe, these people even directed some of that disdain directly at me, a child of primary school age? Yet these people were our so-called friends.

As the years went on, I continued to observe the dynamics in these families, their lives, the choices, and the career paths their children took. There was an interesting correlation, a pattern of what I heard as a child and the paths many in the family ended up taking.

With all other things being equal, those who treated me with kindness and respect, who lovingly looked after me while in their care, who never said a harsh word about my parents, tended to have what we would consider a typical family— not perfect, but they had it mostly together. As for the big talkers, with their lavish suburban lifestyles and big promotions, the ones who would disparage my family, many ended up with a sad history of divorce, some with family violence, drug abuse and even suicide.

The more I observed as the years rolled on, my respect and admiration for the character of my parents and what they sacrificed and passed on were invaluable in a thousand ways, more than I could imagine. It was a valuable gift that was being cultivated and would serve me well later in life.

Learning to Lead

In time, I slowly became aware of my own quirkiness. I realised that I saw the world through a lens of logic and patterns. At the same time, the focus of my journey became understanding and connecting with people to learn what makes them tick and to navigate this social minefield. I became motivated.

My first professional job was with a major telco as a young technical officer in digital data network design. Inadequate, vulnerable, insecure and inexperienced as I was, I quickly discovered how deficient I was for the role. It was like being dropped in a jungle with no map. I had to learn to survive – and fast.

I also needed to grow and overcome my anxieties. So, I took a calculated risk. Four years after joining the telco, I decided to leave the stable, well-paid job, and go it alone. I was in my early twenties, so I figured if things didn't work out, I could still return.

I wish I had the space to tell you the whole story – but I was on my way to retiring in less than ten years, the flow of money was that good. But just over a year later, the world collapsed around me as we were hit with a recession – "the recession we had to have." It was the '90s. The bills piled up and the savings eventually dried up as the nation clung to every dollar.

The irony was that I saw the patterns of a looming recession early. I knew it was coming before "recession" was ever echoed through the media. It was the ability to recognise certain patterns that I was learning to understand. It was one of those insights that we still talk about to this day. But for whatever reason, I didn't prepare. I felt like a fool.

But what I lost in money, I gained in experience, and anyone who's been there knows that this type of education is not cheap, but it can change your life — the priceless kind of education. It helped me gain knowledge about entrepreneurship and management, but also allowed me to conquer my social anxieties and connect with various professionals from diverse industries, including the corporate and finance sectors, and with private business owners.

At the same time, I was accepting leadership roles in the community. I was also becoming involved in several areas within my local church, working mainly with youth and young adults. I served on several committees, some of which had a vast generation gap between myself and the senior leadership. In some cases, the gap was more than thirty years. I also had the privilege of serving as director of a Scout-like youth club called Pathfinders. For several years, I learned to lead a club with more than 40 children, a dozen staff and all the politics associated with dealing with parents. For an Aspie, this was a social minefield. If it wasn't for a fantastic team, the support of the church community and my girlfriend – later my wife – I really don't think I would have endured. The support made all the difference. A few years later, I was invited to serve on the Pathfinder advisory committee for all clubs in the state. It was a real honour.

Looking back, I can hardly believe that those older, wiser and significantly more experienced leaders saw any potential in me. Somehow they did, and that fearful start set me on a path to a variety of leadership experiences that would eventually help me reimagine what it would mean to be a Wholehearted Leader.

Discerning Leadership

As time went on, I interacted with various leaders worldwide, from diverse disciplines and backgrounds, from those at the highest level of politics, heads of industry, the powerful and wealthy, to influential community organisers and many leaders of faith. I have been able to observe how they lead and treat their staff, teams and subordinates, watching their achievements and, more importantly, what they leave behind when they move on.

It was identical to what I observed within the families growing up as a child, but on a larger scale. Like the journey through a Rube Goldberg machine that navigates its path with all the gears, levers and spinners working successfully to an end, it was an obvious pattern that those in leadership who are happiest and most content often share a set of common values. In one way or another, they place the people they lead ahead of themselves. Their energies are focused on adding value to the people and the community they lead. They are teachable, humble, and often self-sacrificing. Their teams develop camaraderie, respect and dignity for each other, which is increasingly lacking in today's world. Their marriages are usually more stable, and their children are close, mature and often better behaved. This is no coincidence — it's as clear a pattern as you can get.

If the ability to see patterns was the tool, then the values became the driving motivation for me. I was discovering what it takes to build strong communities and be exceptional leaders.

I understand that profits are paramount in running any business — otherwise, why have a business? But when employees feel valued and respected, they are more likely to go above and beyond in their work and treat their peers and customers with the same level of care. A company that emphasises a strong culture of inclusivity and support for employees will be rewarded with not only increased productivity and job satisfaction, but also with positive results in terms of loyalty, from employees and customers. Prioritising profits may be important, but it shouldn't come at the expense of valuing and investing in the people who make the business successful in the first place.

Over the years, I have observed more and more companies that have decided to take a different approach, one that values people in a way that very few do. This creates an environment of self-worth and dignity, which cultivates a community of workers that either already have, or are developing, the values that inspire and empower a new generation of leaders. It's a change driven by new priorities, especially in a post-pandemic world, which has not only redefined the work-life balance but also brought a shift in attitude, mindset and behaviour that continues to grow and expand from the workplace into the communities in which we live.

Consider just a few contemporary examples:

Semco: a Brazilian industrial company that promotes employee autonomy and with no traditional organisational charts, job titles or traditional hierarchies. Employees choose their own salaries, set their own schedules and have a say in company decisions. These employees have access to all financial and operational information, which gives everyone a clear understanding of how the business operates with complete transparency. If this seems counterintuitive – it will for many of us – consider that Semco has become one of Brazil's most successful industrial companies. Do a search for "Ricardo Semler," Semco's founder – his influence has been global.

Morning Star: a US-based tomato-processing company that operates without managers or hierarchy. Its employees work autonomously, without any top-down directives. This approach creates a collaborative and innovative work culture in which people can improve their skills and capabilities. It has helped Morning Star become a leader in the tomato-processing industry, with a reputation for quality products and a strong commitment to its employees.

Buurtzorg: a Dutch healthcare company with a self-managed team structure. Rather than relying on traditional top-down management, its nurses are empowered to manage themselves and make important decisions about patient care. The company's innovative approach has been a resounding success, leading to improved patient outcomes and higher levels of job satisfaction. The company's unique approach has earned it a global reputation as an innovative leader in healthcare.

FAVI: a French automotive parts manufacturer that practises worker participation in decision-making and profit-sharing. The company's unique model is built around the idea that employees are critical stakeholders who should have a voice in the work they do and share in the success of the business. This approach encourages workers to take a long-term view of the company's success rather than focusing solely on short-term gains. The company's innovative approach has earned it worldwide recognition for its commitment to employee well-being, collaboration and responsible leadership.

Spotify: a Swedish music-streaming company that focuses on team autonomy and collaboration. The company promotes regular communication and knowledge-sharing across teams, fostering a culture of learning and ongoing improvement. This helps prevent silos forming within the organisation and supports the continual development of products and services. This approach has been key to Spotify's success in the highly competitive music-streaming industry.

For the politician, it's prioritising citizens' needs over the interests of corporations and other influential groups.

For industry giants, it's balancing profits and responsibilities towards society and the environment.

For the manager, it's leading by example, cultivating a positive work culture and empowering employees to reach their potential.

For the spouse, it's building a strong and healthy relationship based on mutual respect, communication and trust, making time for each other despite life's challenges and demands.

For the parent, it's providing emotional and financial support, acting as a positive role model and prioritising quality time with the children.

For the leader, it's setting a vision, inspiring and motivating others to achieve it, being accountable for results, and continually learning and adapting to changing circumstances.

For the Wholehearted Leader, it's leading with authenticity, vulnerability and empathy, fostering a culture of trust and belonging, and valuing the humanity of every person on the team.

Adopting my Mum's Superpower

Today I mainly work in the background, occasionally taking on leadership roles, speaking engagements or leading teams in different areas. But my greatest fulfilment lies in helping others explore their potential and mentoring their growth as possible future leaders. The pleasure comes from recognising potential in others, discovering their unique traits, and seeing them grow and succeed, not only in their professional lives but primarily within their families.

Apart from navigating the business-tech sector daily, I spend my free time working within the community and the humanitarian field, building bridges within the interfaith community, and connecting with politicians where appropriate. I treasure the time spent with those on the margins of society, the homeless, the poor, the struggling mother, the drug addict – those wounded in so many ways. When they tell their stories, their abuse and often their struggles with depression, the old maxim always haunts me: "There, but for the grace of God, go I." Although they might be wounded, I can see beauty beneath their pain and witness kindness beneath their scars. Moreover, remarkable talents, abilities and even brilliance lie within.

The work we do has a positive impact on many in diverse ways, but we experience the greatest benefits through personal transformation beyond our imagination. The influence of our efforts can extend beyond our lifetime, touching not only those close to us but also our descendants for generations. These humbling experiences put into perspective the importance of recognising the immeasurable value of every person.

Did Mum have a special gift, a talent, something unique or rare? She was no artist, mathematician or musician, yet she had a rare quality that imperceptibly moved throughout the community. Through her actions, she led by example, and made a difference in people's lives, tenderly helping them navigate through unfamiliar waters. How many children of those parents, now parents or grandparents themselves, have a better life or a happier home because of some tiny seed of compassion, care and hope that Mum planted? She quietly stepped out and made a difference in her sphere of influence. Led by her values, her contribution was in giving a little of her time to support, show kindness and accept people as they were.

Like a giant oak, change begins with a seed, often in the form of a kind gesture or act of empowerment and mentorship, then blossoms within our circle of influence. By prioritising people over power, principles over prestige, and ethics over money, these are the patterns I've observed and the values that can truly make a difference in our communities.

That's leadership – and it changes people's lives.

ABOUT THE AUTHOR
John Smilek

John Smilek is an accomplished CIO with more than 30 years' experience in the business-technology sector. Throughout his career, he has served on numerous councils and advisory committees. He has gained a reputation for his unique ability to identify patterns that are often missed, and which enables him to anticipate outcomes.

In addition to his work, John is known for his strong commitment to community building and interfaith relations. During his free time, he frequently connects with local councils, state and federal officials, community organisers and humanitarian organisations, working tirelessly to build bridges across diverse communities.

John's exceptional skills and knowledge have also led to frequent invitations to speak, teach, and instruct others across his broad range of experience. He is passionate about sharing his expertise and helping communities to thrive through collaboration and cooperation.

He is happily married with two sons and cherishes every moment with them. John is also an avid reader and can often be found buried in a good book or indulging in sports and adventurous activities such as snowboarding, skiing, hockey, hiking and even skateboarding.

CONNECT WITH JOHN

LinkedIn: *www.linkedin.com/in/johnsmilek*

www.ingramcontent.com/pod-product-compliance
Lightning Source LLC
Chambersburg PA
CBHW022015290426
44109CB00015B/1176